Whose Hands Are These?

Whose Hands Are These?

A Gifted Healer's Miraculous True Story

GENE EGIDIO

WARNER BOOKS

A Time Warner Company

The information offered in this book is not intended as a substitute for medical advice. If you think you may have a medical problem, you are advised to seek the help of a qualified health care professional.

Throughout this book some names and descriptions have been slightly altered out of respect for the privacy of my family, friends, and clients.

Copyright © 1997 by Gene Egidio
All rights reserved.

Warner Books, Inc., 1271 Avenue of the Americas,
New York, NY 10020

W A Time Warner Company

First Printing: August 1997
10 9 8 7 6 5 4 3 2 1

Library of Congress Cataloging-in-Publication Data
Egidio, Gene
    Whose hands are these? / Gene Egidio.
        p.   cm.
    ISBN 0-446-52045-4
    1. Psychic surgery.   2. Mental healing.   3. Spiritual healing.
4. Egidio, Gene.   I. Title.
RZ400.E47   1997
615.8'52--dc20   96-29125
                                                            CIP

Book design by Maura Gibbons

To my children, Diane, Annie, Victoria, and John; my sisters, Antonette and Anna Marie; my brother, Dominic; and to my sweetheart Elaine. Also to all my friends who made this endeavor possible.

ACKNOWLEDGMENTS

I would like to take this opportunity to thank Genevieve Crane, for her tireless work in the creation of this book; and Rani Stoler, for her expertise and wisdom that guided me through the process of bringing this book to life. I would also like to extend my thanks to Yabo and Yolande, to Elsie and all the people who added to the success of this book, and to those who silently helped but have chosen to remain anonymous.

CONTENTS

Preface

You will find this book by Gene Egidio warmly human and inspiring, a delight to read, and at the same time a manual for your own personal development. Gradually it will awaken within you growing faith in your own power to heal yourself. Essentially it is a story of not only one man's exceptional ability to heal others, but also the power in all human beings to tune in to the divine consciousness within them. In this emphasis on the universality of the healing gift, Gene demonstrates himself to be a true spiritual healer.

We live in an age of growing awareness of energy as the underlying reality of the material universe. Matter, as physics has shown, is energy. The more mankind advances in this awareness, the more people will come to understand that true healing is not so much a process of killing disease as of strengthening the body's energy defenses.

For this human body is not what it seems. Though superficially a composite of bones, organs, and fleshly tissues, on a deeper level of reality it is composed of energy—countless vortices of it, working together in harmony if the body is well. If we are unwell, it is primarily because our energy is low, or because these vortices of energy are out of sync with each other.

Gene shows us that this energy can be strengthened and brought into harmony, both within the body and in the body's relationship with our environment. He helps people to do that, as he has helped over a hundred of them here too, at my home called Crystal Hermitage. Above all, he helps them learn to help themselves, and to grow in faith and love.

—J. Donald Walters
author of *The Path* and *Secrets of Life*

Introduction

I have been giving healing energy to people for over a decade, and in this time many people have asked me many questions. Invariably, the one question that always comes up is, "How did you start doing healing work?"

The path that led me to healing was a strange one, with many unexpected twists and turns. In the pages that follow I'm going to share with you the events that shaped my life and took me on this unexpected journey.

This was not a journey I had wanted to take. In fact I avoided it for nearly half a century, but finally I could repress my healing gift no longer. The comfortable life I had built for myself as a middle-class householder was turned upside down and inside out, and I was faced with the realization that the old way no longer worked. It was time for me to walk on an uncharted path. At first I halfheartedly embraced this new way of life, even treating it as a hobby, but with the passing of time my respect and understanding of this gift increased. I found that I could send healing energy to people. This energy creates a subliminal state, where the body and mind are put in a state of bliss, and this in turn ignites the life force. If the person has the will to get well, he or she will then be able to continue the healing process with their own energy. This process is not unlike jump-starting a car battery. Although the battery has insufficient energy to start the car's engine, once a certain amount of energy from an outside source is transferred, the car starts and can rely on its own resources to reach its destination.

I began to see how my healing abilities could be used to help mankind, and now I am dedicated to this cause. It has become my life's work.

As I live ever increasingly in the present moment, it is quite difficult for me to remember past events. However, from time to time, I have flashes of things that happened to me in my childhood and teenage years, as well as my early adult life. I believe that the experiences I remember and which shaped my life are revealed to me for the purpose of sharing past events with those who wish to know my story.

We all have different paths to travel; some of us go through life looking for our path. I think I'm one of the fortunate ones, for I know what path I am to take, and I am now totally focused on carrying out this work and reaching as many people as possible. My goal in this life is to complete this mission, even though obstacles arise from time to time to challenge me. I am sitting in this vehicle called the human body, which sometimes does not want to cooperate with me, but I know I have to do this, so I try to get this vehicle to support my needs so I can continue the work. I believe it is my duty to spread the healing energy and light to everyone who wishes to experience it.

Many people are led to believe that healing is a fascinating occupation. It certainly does have some uplifting and surprising moments; however, like any other work, it is not without its own set of problems. At times the energy I work with is so strong that it burns my hands and leaves blisters, not to mention the discomfort my body experiences from the intense heat. It is similar to being in an overheated room with no thermostat to adjust. And sometimes this energy force is so strong that I have to stop it, for fear that it will short out my physical vehicle. This gift is not a child's toy to play with, but rather requires a great amount of dedication, respect, understanding, and responsibility in handling the ways in which it can be used.

When I embraced this occupation I gave up a considerable amount of privacy that most people take for granted, for there is a constant barrage of telepathic messages coming at me from all over the world at all times of the day and night. This causes my work to become a twenty-four-hour-a-day job. I'm like a 7-Eleven store, always open for business, but I accept that because the healing energy is always there, and I am blessed, for I usually need very little sleep. As I continue to walk on this path, I will try to reach as many people as possible in the time allotted to me to do this work. I'm here to serve all mankind and heal the pain and suffering.

I now live in Southern California. When I'm not traveling, I do healings at my two centers: one in Encinitas, in the county of San Diego, and the other in Santa Monica, in Los Angeles County. I also am giving seminars to persons who wish to explore personal development or ask the age-old question, Why are we here? I believe it is very important to do as much as we can to help ourselves and our planet evolve. I also devote one day a week to doing phone healings and photo healings for those who do not have easy access to my centers. For more information about me and my work you can send a fax or a self-addressed stamped envelope to:

Gene Egidio
Breakthru Institute of Awareness
575 Second Street
Encinitas, California 92024 USA
Tel: (760) 436-0220
Fax: (760) 436-1391

You may also check my homepage on the World Wide Web or contact me by e-mail:
www.egidio.org
e-mail: GeneEgidio@worldnet.att.net

I leave my love and peace with you.

Section One

The U.S.S.R.

It was a warm summer night in July 1989. I was scheduled to catch the midnight train, so I quickened my pace. I, Gene Egidio, an average middle-class American, was in the Soviet Union for the first time and was about to catch the Moscow-to-Leningrad express. When I entered the Moscow train station, I felt as if I were instantly transported back into the 1930s. The station was dimly lit, the interior drab and dismal. The cars were antiquated, and it was obvious the facilities were not at all up to Western standards. I turned to look back at the waiting-room area and suddenly became aware that the atmosphere was threatening. There were soldiers everywhere, with pistols and submachine guns, and I had the distinct feeling that they were all watching me and saying, Make one wrong move, Buddy, and you've had it. We're just waiting to nab you.

As a child growing up in Cold War America, I'd been told that the Soviet Union was the enemy and we were the "good guys." Now, I wasn't a child—this was real life, and I was thinking, Gene, how did you get yourself into this? Just then my Russian interpreter, Maria Norovski, dropped her bag next to mine.

She was a tall, slender woman in her late thirties with long brown hair, worn in a French twist. She dressed conservatively: dark colors, no jewelry, and just a trace of makeup. Maria could have easily passed as a schoolmarm or nun and, as it turned out, she had taught school long before she became an interpreter.

"We must find our car now," she said, in her clipped, official English. "We will be boarding in twenty minutes."

I followed Maria down the platform until she stopped in front of a car marked with an enormous number 13 that immediately triggered my superstitious side. Ominous feelings were flickering through my mind until I glanced into Maria's smiling face. "Isn't it wonderful," she said. "Thirteen—a lucky number in Russia!" I returned her grin and laughed. Moments later a serene peace swept over me and I settled back for our eight-hour trip. In my heart of hearts, I knew that everything would be all right.

Just before the train pulled out there was a knock on the door of our sleeper. When I opened it there stood a tall, robust man in his late forties. He launched into a volley of words, his dark eyes flashing, as he pointed to the top bunk and waved his ticket. Since I didn't speak Russian, I turned to Maria for an explanation. With a shrug of her shoulders and an air of resignation, she told me that it was not unusual for strangers to share a compartment. "This is the Soviet Union," she said. "Everything is shared here."

I nodded my understanding and with a smile motioned him to take the top bunk. When he passed me I sensed a great pain. There was nothing external, but I immediately knew the problem was on the left side of his face.

Through Maria he introduced himself as Gregor Kinoshka. Kinoshka explained that he had been in Chernobyl during the explosion and was caught in the radiation. He then opened his mouth and showed us a cancerous hole in his gum.

Through Maria, I told our new compartment companion that I was a healer and that I had intuitively felt the pain he was experiencing. Another short conversation volleyed between them and he smiled.

"Please," Maria said, "he asked if you would help him and work on him." I assured him that I would.

By this time the train had left the station, so we were swaying back and forth and it got pretty funny. I was standing on the two bottom bunks, holding on with one hand to steady myself, while trying to put my other hand on the area of his face where I felt his pain.

"Now, there's nothing to be afraid of," I said. "I can help you, Gregor, but the trick is for me not to fall and kill the both of us." I said this in English, but we both saw the humor in the situation and laughed.

I held my hand on his jaw for about two to three minutes, until I sensed his energy field expanding. Then I held my hand about two inches above his jaw and gradually pulled my hand away as I could see and feel his energy field radiating out from his body. My companion, Inga, and Maria were both watching with amused looks; I realized I probably looked like a juggler trying to do a delicate balancing act.

When I saw that his energy field had extended out from his body twelve to eighteen inches, I stopped and shortly afterward he closed his eyes and nodded off. I returned to my bunk, but I was too energized to sleep and spent the better part of the night in the swaying passageway talking to Maria.

I was grateful that she too was a night owl. Her English was fluent, with almost no accent, so it was easy for us to converse. Maria asked a lot of questions; not only was she curious about me because I was an American, but she wanted to know how I did the healing work.

"How did you find out you had the ability to heal?" she asked.

"I had the good fortune to be born with this gift," I replied. "However, it took me fifty years to accept and to realize what I could do with it."

"Did your parents have the same gift?"

"My mother did," I replied, "but she didn't use it because she knew my father would object."

"You know, the Russian people consider a person with your gift very special."

"It doesn't belong to me," I said, "but it's mine to pass along to others. That's the reason I'm here: I felt compelled to come to Russia and give my gift to the Russian people."

"I'm very touched that you want to help," she said, "especially since our countries hardly ever see eye to eye on any issue."

I nodded in understanding. I wanted to tell her about my vision and mission at the Piskarovskoye Cemetery, but decided to save that for our arrival.

After chatting with her for the better part of the night, we finally decided to try to take a nap before we got to Leningrad.

I had lapsed into a semiconscious state when the sound of someone crying woke me. I opened my eyes and looked up to see Gregor sitting up in his bunk with tears streaming down his face. I turned to Maria with alarm and concern; she too was crying.

"What's wrong?" I said. "What's going on?"

She shook her head and spoke through her tears. "Nothing is wrong. I just had a conversation with our friend, and he said something that touched my heart."

"What did he say?" I asked.

"He said that he had been suffering tremendous pain ever since Chernobyl, but now he felt no pain at all. When he tried to stick his tongue into the hole in his gum, he couldn't find it. It wasn't there—it felt as if someone had sewn it up. That in itself is a miracle." She continued as her eyes held me tightly: "He said that he had been a Communist for over forty years, and today was the first day he realized there was a God."

Just to hear this man say, to a total stranger, that he believed in God was worth all the trials and tribulations of this trip. After exchanging very happy smiles and satisfied nods, all four of us ended up taking another nap.

The conductor's announcement in Russian—"Leningrad, Leningrad! Thirty minutes!"—woke us up.

I stirred out of my slumber and sat pensively watching our approach into the city, reflecting on the reason for my visit and the importance of the mission that had brought me here to Leningrad.

Before getting off the train, Gregor reached into his small satchel, pulled out three apples, and told Maria, "These apples are from my own tree. I would like to give them to you and your friends as a token of my appreciation."

Fruit, I learned, was a precious commodity in the Soviet Union and not easy to come by, but he had shared what he had with us. The gesture meant a lot to me; I felt very honored to receive this gift. As our eyes met, I knew I had touched a heart. I felt a deep satisfaction and I smiled when I said, "Thank you."

When we got off the train, we were welcomed by a group of people. Among them was a photographer/reporter from the Tass news service. News apparently travels very fast in the Soviet Union: He already knew about the healing I had done on the train and wanted a story. As I was pondering this lightning response, Gregor ran to the reporter and, smiling and talking excitedly, told him about the miracle the American had worked.

My interpreter was introducing me to the reporter when a Russian couple, Dmitri and Katrina Sakalow, approached us.

They were relatives of a client I had in California and had agreed to organize my stay in Leningrad. We exchanged nods and handshakes and, with Maria's help, spent some time in polite small talk until I drew a deep breath, smiled, and said, "I need to go to Piskarovskoye Cemetery."

"Why do you want to go there?" my astounded hosts asked. "How do you even know about it?"

"I feel that I'm compelled to be there," I said. At that time I did not want to tell them why I had flown halfway around the world for the specific purpose of visiting that cemetery.

"It is such a dreary day that it might be better to go straight to our destination," Maria said, and I knew by the tone of her voice that she intended to discourage the trip.

"Is there a possibility of a bad storm?" I asked, looking at the gray sky.

"Probably not."

"Well then, I would really like to go there this morning."

With that, Maria told Katrina and Dmitri our decision. They said they would be happy to drive us to the cemetery. I invited the reporter to come with us. He accepted, and off we went, a minicaravan winding its way across the city.

White Nights

The clouds were gray and ominous when we reached the outskirts of the city and there, sprawled in the middle of a residential area, was the Piskarovskoye Memorial Cemetery.

We approached the outer perimeter of the graveyard and walked up seven stone steps that brought us to the top of a platform with an ornate building on either side of us. About fifty yards ahead was an eternal flame, not unlike the one on President John F. Kennedy's grave, and this setting immediately brought to mind the many mental pictures I had seen of the gatekeepers of the next world. I looked around and saw small gatherings of mourners with their heads bowed, as if they were talking to the people who were buried there.

We walked down another flight of steps that led to a long walkway. Although the air of the place was solemn, the beauty was breathtaking. Not only was the lawn carefully manicured, but I could sense it had also been hand-touched with love, and the abundant rose gardens were exquisite. "I don't think I've ever seen a more beautiful cemetery," I said to no one in particular, and realized I was whispering.

I saw a young couple putting flowers near one of the gravestones. The woman was in a long white dress, and the man with her was in a smartly tailored dark dress suit.

"Why are they dressed like that?" I asked Maria.

"They've just gotten married," she replied.

"Why would a wedding couple come to a cemetery?" I asked.

"It is a custom," she said. "When a couple marries in Leningrad, the first stop is to the cemetery to pay their respects to the people who died defending the city during World War Two. Leaving their wedding flowers here is their way of thanking these people for their resistance to the Nazi invasion. Approximately one million people starved to death during this time, and the ones who were fortunate enough to survive were forced to scrape the paste off the wallpaper, then boil and eat it."

She was very moved, and her eyes were glistening as she continued.

"No one forgets what the people of Leningrad endured during the war," she explained. "Not only were we cut off from the rest of the world by the Nazi blockade, but we were cut off from the rest of the Soviet Union as well. Hitler had ordered the city to be wiped off the face of the earth and formed a tight blockade, bombing it until it was leveled to the ground."

"Those were trying times for everyone on this planet," I said, "but not everyone suffered as greatly as these people."

She nodded solemnly.

As I started walking down the path, I could sense the incredible amount of sadness that still lingered here, so much so that I could feel my legs getting heavy as I walked farther into the cemetery. I looked to my right and left and saw gravestones that had only the years 1941–1944 written on them. I later found out these were the mass graves of the civilians and soldiers who had died during the 900-day siege. One person out of every four of Leningrad's population had been killed; half a million people were buried in these mass graves.

As I continued down the path, I could make out the soft facial features of a woman carved into a large granite statue.

She was approximately twenty-five or thirty feet tall, her arms extended out holding a wreath of oak leaves in a gesture of welcome and compassion. She was the Lady of the Motherland, the symbol of Eternal Glory. The oak leaves that flowed from one hand to the other gave me the feeling that this was the link between her heart and the heart of all the people of the Soviet Union.

As I drew closer to the statue I quickened my pace, wanting to be alone for a moment. I was now approximately twenty-five feet ahead of the rest of the group. I climbed up the steps that surrounded the statue, and down to the other side, behind it. There, carved in stone, were the words by a Leningrad poet, Olga Bergholts:

> *Here lie the people of Leningrad,*
> *Here are the citizens — men, women and children . . .*
> *They gave their lives*
> *Defending you, Leningrad,*
> *Cradle of Revolution.*
> *We cannot number all their noble names here,*
> *So many lie beneath the eternal granite,*
> *But of those honored by this stone,*
> *Let no one forget*
> *Let nothing be forgotten.*

I was alone now, and it was time to do what I had come halfway around the world to do.

I was here because of an insight I had received one night after an American businessman came to my healing center in California. He had spent a considerable amount of time in the Soviet Union. When he came to me he was very distraught.

After I had worked on him, he got off the table and said, "Oh, I feel so relaxed now. You should go to the Soviet Union. You're what they need."

"Oh no, I'm absolutely not interested in going there," I answered matter-of-factly. "What's there, with the Communists in charge?"

However, that night I received an impregnable insight of great pain and suffering, and knew that my talent was needed in Russia, specifically to help facilitate the release of a dark energy. My mind's eye flashed on millions of tortured souls being kept earthbound, trapped between time and space.

So the comfort of staying put, in sunny California, was not to be.

Less than three months after receiving this message I was here in a cemetery in Leningrad for the purpose of releasing those many tortured souls. As I walked back from behind the statue, Inga approached me. I went to her and put my arm on her shoulder for support. The emotions of the souls buried here caught up with me; I became weak and began to cry.

I simultaneously experienced deep feelings of sadness, anger, despair, hunger, hopelessness, and the agonizing torment that these poor people had experienced before their deaths. I could actually *see* the incredible suffering these people had endured.

Because of the horrific way these people had died their souls did not know they were without bodies. They were being held to this point on Earth and were experiencing their death over and over, caught between time and space, because their transition from life to death had been so traumatic. (I should explain here that souls are records of our lifetimes. They are energy, and if they think they are in a living body, they remain earthbound. Part of my gift allows me to release earthbound souls; it was time for these souls to move on, and I'd come to facilitate this.)

After I gained my composure, I said, "Well, Inga, it's been done. It's all over." As I said this, I could feel the release in my own body. It felt as if forty or fifty pounds of weight had been lifted from my shoulders. The extreme sadness I had been experiencing turned into happiness and I continued to cry, but now I was crying tears of joy.

I could feel a loving energy flowing freely in the vicinity of the statue. I could sense that the mood had been transformed into one of serenity and peacefulness. The heavens must have felt this release too, because the sun abruptly peeked through the gray clouds and, within ten to fifteen minutes, the sky cleared and it became a bright sunny afternoon.

When I glanced up I saw the members of my group coming toward me. Their faces showed expressions of alarm and concern over my emotional outbreak. I needed to have this experience in my own private space and held up my hand, telling them not come any closer. They turned and walked respectfully to the other side of the statue.

After resting awhile I felt myself returning to some semblance of normality and looked at Inga, who was standing quietly nearby, giving me her moral support.

"You know, Inga, in today's rational world we all need a reality check, and the proof of what has just happened here will be evident very shortly in the form of birds. There will be many birds flying over the statue in groups of threes and fours."

Inga looked at me strangely, as if to say, Have you lost your marbles? But, good friend that she was, she smiled and patted my shoulder. Just then I gazed up at the fluffy white clouds in the pale blue sky.

"There they are," I said, "just as I envisioned them!" I saw one bird, then two, three, and within fifteen minutes there were literally thousands of birds flying overhead.

I think this was one of the few times in my healing career that I wasn't surprised. I knew the released souls would manifest themselves in the form of birds in every shape and size imaginable, flying in random patterns in groups of threes and fours and, oddly enough, they were flying out from behind the statue where I had gone to do the release. As they flew out they turned, flew directly over the statue's head, and then departed the cemetery.

The physical manifestation was spectacular.

Everyone was baffled. They were pointing at the sky and talking loudly among themselves. No one knew where the birds had come from or where they were going, nor could they identify them.

The photojournalist from Tass didn't know what was going on either, but like any reporter anywhere in the world he smelled a good story, whipped out his camera, and started filming. Now the proof of what I had done was captured on film, there for all to see.

As is always the case, when something happens that people don't understand, they become frightened, and the unexplained phenomenon of the birds did create fear in my companions. "There is really nothing to fear," I said, sensing their apprehension. "There is nothing more that needs to be done here, and I think we should leave the cemetery now." My friends breathed a sigh of relief and quickly headed to their cars.

I was told later that the birds flew over the cemetery for three days and then disappeared just as abruptly as they had appeared.

After we left the Piskarovskoye Memorial Cemetery, we continued on to the home of our host and hostess, the Sakalows. After weaving our way across the city again, the car finally came to a halt in front of a red-brick apartment house that looked as if it had been there forever.

As we stepped into the hallway I spotted an elevator that could only be described as tiny. I was looking at it dubiously, when Dmitri motioned for me to get in.

"Does this thing really go up?" I asked.

Maria laughed. "Don't worry, it has been taking people up and down since the Revolution."

Again my host motioned for me to get in and I obliged. Incredibly, he squeezed in beside me, wiggled, smiled, and closed the door behind him. Sure enough, with a creaking laboring noise and a sudden lurch, the elevator started moving upward. I had the mental image of being in a barrel and being slowly hoisted to the top by someone on the ground, heaving and pulling a rope. We inched slowly upward until the elevator reached the seventh floor. Dmitri opened the door and we stepped into a hallway badly in need of paint.

The large wooden door opened directly into a living room, which looked like something found in most American homes in the first quarter of this century. There were lace doilies, statuettes, and little knick-knacks everywhere. The walls were covered with family photographs, dating back two or three generations.

Dmitri motioned to the couch, indicating that I should sit and wait until the others got to his apartment. The atmosphere was a little awkward, but I sat politely and quietly. When everyone reached the apartment we were invited into the dining room for a late-afternoon lunch.

There was a large table with a beautifully embroidered linen tablecloth. The table was elegantly set, with delicate china plates, long-stemmed crystal glasses, and intricately patterned silverware.

The contrast between the elegant table setting and the actual dinner being served was striking. The food that the Sakalows served on silver trays still held the shape of the tin cans it came in. Spam was left untouched in its container so that it would be recognized for the delicacy that it was. I was touched by the sincerity and humanity of these gentle people. (I later found out from Maria that both Dmitri and Katrina had gone to each family in the building, asking them to donate a can of something, so they could have enough food to feed us.)

After lunch, when we returned to the living room for conversation and tea, there was a knock at the door. When Dmitri opened the door, a woman carrying her small son entered and, through Maria, I learned that the child could not walk.

"How old is the boy?" I asked as I took him into my arms.

"Two," was the reply.

"Is there a bed I can lay him on? I want to work on him."

Our hostess motioned for me to follow her.

I worked on Nicolas for about fifteen minutes, until he fell into a gentle sleep, then I returned to the living room to rejoin the conversation.

After an hour or so we heard the boy crying; he'd wet the bed I would be sleeping in that night. After his mother changed him, I suggested she stand him up in front of her, extend her arms to the child, and let him walk toward her while she held on to him. She then turned him loose and he started walking normally on his own. The mother burst into tears and the others started to laugh and cry. Dmitri let out a loud scream of joy, and a great warmth came over me.

I knew then that there was no difference between people in the way they expressed joy and happiness and, as I've said many times since, there really is no difference in any of us: We all have the same problems, the same fears and conflicts, the same joys.

That evening, Dmitri and Katrina invited some people to come to their apartment. I thought I'd be dealing with twenty or thirty, but once again Russian word-of-mouth produced a substantially larger number of people. When seventy-five people showed up, I decided I would hold an Open Eye Meditation.

I found early in my healing career that the Open Eye Meditation was an effective way of transmitting energy to many people in a short length of time. This is a meditation that begins like most meditations, by having people sit erect, take a few deep breaths, and slowly exhale. If they feel uncomfortable with it I invite them to close their eyes. When I sense that everyone is relaxed, I transfer the healing energy that runs through my eyes to each and every person in the room. I do this by making eye contact and, whether their eyes are opened or closed, the energy gets through.

As I transfer the healing energy from one person to another the energy level in the entire room increases dramatically. It's like cranking up the volume on a powerful stereo amplifier. When the sound is turned up and people reach a higher plateau, they can see the energy. The most common manifestation is being able to see a collage of colors, changes within my face, or large bright auras around me. Others see the entire room filling up with a bright white light.

I want to pause here to explain how energy is seen. It is similar to what happens if you throw a bucket of water on a tree. When the water hits the solid object, it splashes off. In other words, you see the liquid flying away from the body in a scattering motion. As these "splashes" of energy vibrate from body to body, they raise the vibrations of every person in the room. While the audience is watching me, all of them can "see," or become aware of, situations in their own lives in which work needs to be done; or they might "see" someone in their lives who needs to be dealt with; or "see" the presence of someone who has passed on; or just "see" problematic situations that need answers. This energy works on multiple levels—physical, emotional, mental, and spiritual. All who participate in the Open Eye Meditation will get what they need from it.

The Meditation that evening was a success but, all during the evening, I could sense an uneasiness in Maria.

"Is something wrong?" I asked her after the meeting.

"Was there something about the Meditation that made you uncomfortable?"

"No, no. Why do you ask?" she said.

"Because during the meeting I kept picking up your tension."

It was a moment before she answered. "That's probably due to the fact that we are breaking the law. I'm afraid of the consequences if you get caught."

Totally baffled, I asked, "How am I breaking the law?"

"Without permission from the State, a gathering of more than four people is illegal in the Soviet Union. They will lock you up if they catch you."

I shook my head in disbelief.

"And make no mistake, the law *will* be enforced if someone reports this meeting. The fact that you are an American won't keep you out of serious trouble."

It never occurred to me that holding an Open Eye Meditation would cause a problem. I just knew that what we were doing was totally accepted on a higher level—I was doing what needed to be done. The Meditation, in my opinion, was a success.

"Well, what's done is done," I said.

A moment later a woman stood up and said she would like to relate what she'd seen in her mind's eye during the Meditation. "I saw a cemetery," she said, "and many beautiful birds flying over it."

"Did you go to Piskarovskoye today?" I asked.

"No."

I proceeded to tell her about the extraordinary events of the day. When I finished my story everyone was weeping.

I had left Los Angeles for the Soviet Union with only enough money to get me as far as Germany. My friend Inga, a German-born nurse, knew many dedicated people in the healing field and assured me that they could help raise the money needed to get us to Russia. By doing a number of healings at our first stop in Europe, we made enough to continue on to Moscow. Inga's friend Horst Günther, a Reiki master, and his wife, Edith, accepted me and my work without question. They also made it possible for us to get our plane tickets with no waiting period through a travel agent who was very adept at dealing with the bureaucracy.

While in Germany I reflected on the many Germans killed in Leningrad and realized why Inga's friends were eager to support my efforts to get to Russia. I realized that by releasing the dense vibrations that held both Soviet and German souls earthbound, the need to continue suffering was eliminated, allowing energy to flow freely. This release may well have been the catalyst for some of the historical events that took place a few months later, such as the tearing down of the Berlin Wall and the reuniting of families and friends from both sides of the border.

After spending a very pleasant evening laughing and relaxing in the home of Dmitri and Katrina, their guests left and they ushered me into my bedroom. The huge bed dominating the room was covered by a white lace spread and pillows to match. Katrina had changed the linen after Nicolas had wet the bed. I was exhausted, and the bed looked very inviting. I longed to go to sleep, but the excitement of the day, not to mention the newness of the culture, kept me awake.

I walked to the window and stared out at the luminous patterns of light, the aurora borealis or, as the Russians call it, the "White Nights." It was a late summer night but the sky was as bright as high noon. Suddenly, the aurora borealis triggered a memory: bright lights from another time in another room. I remembered momentary panic, and I was aware of bustling activity around me.

I heard someone ask, "Where is the doctor who diagnosed him?"

Another voice said, "We can't wait any longer. We must start immediately. Is the surgeon ready?"

Then a shadow leaned over me and said, "You are going to sleep for a while now." A mask was clamped over my mouth and nose and within seconds everything began to whirl. My vision blurred, the voices around me faded, and I slipped into a state of nothingness.

Moments passed and I was floating up to the ceiling. I had died.

Childhood Remembered

There in Leningrad, gazing out my bedroom window, I clearly remembered the circumstances leading up to my death. I was twelve years old and living in Yonkers, New York. My parents were Italian-Catholic immigrants and fairly strict disciplinarians. I remembered the glee I felt when my father informed me of a decision he and my mother had made.

"We have decided that you are old enough to go to summer camp this year. That is, if you want to go," my father said to me at the dinner table one evening.

"Want to go?" I exclaimed. "I've wanted to go for the last three years!"

"Well, this year we are going to allow it."

"Great!" I was excited about getting to go somewhere alone. At last I was going to get to do things grown-ups do.

Finally the day arrived for me to leave for camp. In reality it was a very short trip—from Yonkers to Hackensack, New Jersey—but for me it was a major event. My parents put me on the bus and told the driver where to let me off. They waved good-bye to me and I was on my way across the George Washington Bridge. All the flurry of activity and excitement made me tired, but I refused to give in and fall asleep, as I wanted to see everything. With the sun shining down on it, the Hudson River, far, far below us, looked like a silvery ribbon, and I could see boats traveling up and down it. This was a sight not to be missed.

There were other boys on the bus headed for camp. It was a place where city kids could experience some of nature's outdoor activities such as hiking, swimming, and canoeing, plus the usual sports of volleyball, basketball, and baseball. There were campfire cookouts and sing-alongs at night. Our time was structured in such a way as to teach us responsibility, and we were expected to make our beds and do some of the chores involved with running a camp. Then we had free time in which we could, while under adult supervision, do whatever we wished. All in all, it was a nice place for young boys to be during the summer months, when there was no school and we were free to be kids.

I remembered waking early on that fateful Sunday morning with the sunlight streaming through the window next to my cot. A dull pain on my right side, which had started the day before, was getting worse. I was scared and suddenly felt the need to be near my mother. I knew if I could just tell her about it she would know what to do.

I'd gone to the camp nurse the day before. "I don't feel well. I have a ache in my side and a stomachache," I said.

"You kids, you overeat and overexercise. Of course you are going to make yourselves sick. The body can't take that kind of treatment. Try resting for a while and you'll be good as new by tomorrow." As she said this she waved me out of her office. My parents had taught me to respect adults and not question their decisions, so I left her office without saying anything more.

A day had passed, and I was *not* as good as new. As I got out of bed, the dull ache became a sharp, stabbing twinge. I didn't know what to do or whom to turn to, so I decided to ignore it. I took my shower, got dressed, and went outside.

"Maybe if I find something to do, I'll forget about the pain," I mumbled to myself.

I went to the lake and thought about taking out a canoe, but the pain was now a steady throbbing ache, so I sat on the pier instead. By lunchtime I was in sheer agony. I discovered that when I bent over and held onto my side the misery lessened. I hobbled to the dining room in this bent-over position. When I reached the hall, I managed to straighten up long enough to walk through the lunch line with my tray and reach a nearby table. I sat down and eased into a crumpled-up position, which momentarily lessened my suffering. After a few mouthfuls of turkey and dressing, I became nauseous and stood up to leave the table.

"Hey, where are you going?" said Ray, a new friend who was sitting beside me. "You haven't finished your lunch. You know the rules, you have to have an empty tray before you can leave."

"I don't feel good," I managed to stammer.

As I started to walk toward the exit of the dining room, the sudden razor-sharp pain that shot through my body was so agonizing that I was unable to move. I faltered momentarily and then collapsed on the floor. Darkness closed in around me.

The next time I opened my eyes I was in a brightly lit room. I looked up and saw several lights shining directly at me. The light was so intense it hurt my eyes. I squinted and my eyes began to tear. I didn't know where I was and panic set in. My side was still hurting and I was very hot.

"Where am I?" I asked someone standing over me.

There was no answer. Then I became aware of the bustling activity around me.

I heard someone ask, "Where is the doctor who diagnosed him?"

Another voice said, "We can't wait. We must start immediately. Is the surgeon ready?"

A wave of queasiness came over me as I felt the sharp jabbing pain in my side.

Then someone leaned over me and said, "You are going to sleep for a while now."

"My side hurts," I said.

Again there was no answer. Instead, a mask was clamped over my mouth and nose.

I experienced the feeling of sheer terror, as I gulped for a breath of fresh air and discovered there was none. As I gasped, I realized there was a strange and mildly unpleasant odor coming from the mask. I didn't know where I was; I didn't know where my parents were; and to make matters worse, I was very hot and very sick. But I didn't have long to contemplate the situation. Within seconds the room began to whirl, my vision became blurry, and the voices around me faded.

I slipped into a state of nothingness.

Moments passed and I was floating up to the ceiling. I looked down and saw people hovering over my body working together frantically. Their movements were very slow, as if they were moving under water.

"Hey, why are you down there, when I am up here on the ceiling?"

No one answered. It slowly sank in that they couldn't hear me.

I began floating out of the room. The lights gradually dimmed until there was total darkness around me, and then I saw a pinpoint of light directly in front of me and felt my body being pulled toward it. With a *swish*, I was instantaneously transported to another place eons away from where I had been just a moment before. This place was outside of time; there was only the present and it was a steady unvarying forever. The vibration of my soul after it left my body had swiftly accelerated and transported me in a flash to this place, guided by the beam of light.

When I emerged from that transportation, there was nothing but brilliant luminous light. This light didn't seem to have a point of origin; it came from everywhere, everything, and everyone. The radiance of it was overwhelming, yet its sparkling brilliance did not hurt my eyes, for I felt myself being absorbed *into* the light. Every cell in my being was filling up with light. I was becoming the light, and along with this transformation came a feeling of total unconditional love for all living creatures. I suddenly understood *everything*. I had absolute knowledge. This enlightenment gave me a feeling of total well-being. I felt complete and whole and knew that everything was the way it should be. A calm serenity filled my being. I felt comfortable here, because I knew I belonged—this was where I had originated.

The people around me were walking through beautiful grass, but not the kind of grass we know on Earth. It was more like a thick carpet that one could sink into, and it felt soft, yet springy. As I went further into the light I became aware of luminous beings floating around me. I knew I was walking, but there was no sensation of movement. I didn't know where I was, as there was no reference point, but that didn't matter.

When my soul left my body it was instantly put on "automatic pilot" and knew exactly where it was going. Some of the energy in this dimension revealed itself to me as physical forms in the shape of human beings, so that my human consciousness could relate to it. I was in sync with this energy these beings were giving and it felt good to be in the midst of it. They motioned to me and I gladly followed. They were communicating with me, yet nothing was spoken. I was aware that I understood all they were revealing to me, and a sense of warm well-being and peaceful happiness settled over me.

I knew I was one with this energy and all its many manifestations. As these light entities continued to communicate soundlessly with me, I began to hear sounds inside my head that surely were the most beautiful sounds ever created, and these sounds were spoken in a voice everyone could understand. A feeling of awe and wonderment permeated my being. To be in an environment of total love and compassion, even for an instant, gave me a feeling of sheer ecstasy which I can only feebly attempt to describe.

It makes one feel like laughing and crying at the same time, and the feelings are very intense because this energy is vibrating at a velocity well beyond the speed of light. This feeling of well-being was all-consuming and I have never since experienced such an overall sense of completion. It was a thousandfold more fulfilling than the most exhilarating experiences that we know while we are in our bodies. When this light energy entered, I had the feeling that my body had totally dissolved in the light and had merged with all that is. I entered into a state of total bliss. Peace, contentment, and exquisite well-being were the only emotions I felt. As I followed the beings in the direction of the ever-increasing brilliant light, I knew that I knew all of them, yet I'd never seen any of them before.

My stay in this place of total unconditional love and absolute knowledge was short-lived however, for I had not yet completed my journey on this planet. Although I had returned home for a moment, it was not time for my soul to fragment into new souls. There were still lessons my present being needed to learn, and they had to be learned on earth.

Suddenly I had the sensation of something grabbing me by the seat of the pants and pulling me backward, away from the beautiful light and through the darkness.

I didn't want to leave. I fought to stay, but within seconds I was returned to the operating room and was on the ceiling again. It felt as if the hose of a vacuum cleaner had attached itself to my soul and I was literally being sucked back into my body. I instantly felt a sensation of heaviness, of being burdened with a body again.

I heard someone say, "We got him back."

Hours later I awoke to a feeling of dull pain and, as I became aware of my surroundings, I saw that there was a tube inserted into my side for drainage. My parents were there, looking rather anxious and worried.

"Your father and I got here as soon as we could," my mother said to me, as she soothed my brow. "You need to rest now. Don't worry, I will be close by."

My father, a stern look on his face, patted my arm before he left the room.

I could hear the doctors in the hall telling my father I would be okay. They told my parents I had had a close call, but they neglected to tell them I had died. "Your son will recover, but because of this operation he will not have a normal childhood. You must not let him take part in any sport activities or games. We had to make a rather large incision to remove the ruptured appendix, so he'll be weak for a long time. If he exerts himself there is a good possibility that he could die."

That was of little concern to me now, as I drifted in and out of sleep. I was far away from the beautiful place I had glimpsed momentarily, and the dim awareness of the loss caused my heart to ache.

I saw various events of my childhood passing before me.

As a child I had been able to predict events and read minds at an early age. As I tuned in on my mother, who was sitting by my bedside in the hospital, I saw in her mind's eye my christening when I was less than a month old. The light shone through the stained-glass windows of the church, framing my mother in a rainbow of colors. She was holding me in her arms and looking down lovingly at me.

The priest asked, "Who will stand for this child as godfather against Lucifer and the powers of evil?"

A man stepped forward and said, "I, Egidio Pasqualie, will stand for this child."

With that, my mother handed me to my godfather. I could feel the awe, admiration, and respect she had for this man and I saw she was remembering a time when he had helped her.

Mother had discovered a tumor in her abdominal area and had gone to him. He put her on his kitchen table in his tiny Brooklyn apartment and worked on her by the laying on of hands until the tumor had disappeared. He had made it possible for me to be born and she, in her gratitude, had asked him to be my godfather.

As I dozed off, I saw Joseph screaming. Joseph was an Old Country Italian, a little man in his seventies who rented the upstairs apartment of our house. When I was five, before I was attending school, I used to climb the stairs to visit him and he would sit me on his lap and peel an apple for me.

"Well, look who's here," said Joseph, when he opened the door to my knock.

"I came to see you."

"Come in, come in. Look at the big red apple I have."

"Are you going to peel it?" I asked.

"Sure, come and sit on my lap and I'll peel it and we will share it." Joseph smiled. He picked me up and sat me on his lap. Then he took the paring knife and started peeling the apple.

This was always an interesting event for me, because Joseph could peel an apple in one continuous strip. It would curl and curl, but it would never break. I was both mesmerized and fascinated to watch this.

When he finished peeling the apple, he cut off a slice and gave it to me. I took it gladly. He watched me eat, then cut a slice for himself. We took turns eating pieces of the apple until we finished it. I always liked being there with Joseph.

Then came the day when the knife slipped and he nearly cut off his thumb.

"Ouch!" He cried out when he saw what he had done.

He dropped the knife, and his thumb started bleeding profusely. Although he had not cut it off completely, the thumb was laid open and attached only by the skin on one side.

I was only five years old at the time, but I instinctively grabbed his wounded thumb and held onto it. When he pushed my hand away, the finger had nearly stopped bleeding, and that frightened him.

"What did you do?" he yelled.

"I tried to make it well," I said.

"How could you do that? You are just a little boy."

"What do you mean?" I asked. "It's better now."

"No! You shouldn't have been able to do that. This is bad, this is very bad!" All his Old Country superstition was pouring out of him.

He pushed me off his lap, grabbed me by the hand, and started pulling me toward the door. Dealing with me became his first priority; he had forgotten all about the wounded thumb which needed immediate attention. "I am going to tell your parents about this. They should know about your evil powers."

He dragged me downstairs. My feelings were deeply hurt and I did not understand why I was being scolded.

He took me into the living room and told my parents what had happened.

My father shrugged it off and teasingly asked, "Joseph, by any chance did you have a glass of wine before you peeled that apple?"

Joseph stood there for a moment and then said, "From now on, my place is off limits to your son. Don't let him come up to see me again." With that he stormed out of our house, and I was never allowed to visit him again.

Joseph's abrupt rejection stung me deeply and I began to cry over the loss of his friendship.

"Why doesn't he like me anymore? I stopped his thumb

from bleeding. Why did that make him so mad?" I asked my mother.

My mother laid her hand on my head, stroked it absent-mindedly, and said nothing.

I looked at my father, but his head was buried in the newspaper.

"We will find other things for you to do," my mother said gently. She tried to let on that nothing was wrong, but I could tell she was concerned.

My mother had the same healing gift I had, but she didn't accept it and rarely did she use it. Only when I was very ill would I be aware of what she was capable of doing. Within moments of her entering my room and caressing me or holding me in her arms, I would start to feel better. I know now that her touch was a hands-on healing. She also had the good fortune of being able to heal herself. I remember when she was hospitalized for a hip replacement, within four days she was out of the hospital and working in her garden.

She knew that I could also heal, but didn't say anything, because she knew my father didn't believe in such things. She knew this was a gift I had been born with, and probably knew what I would eventually do with it, but she never discussed it with me, or anyone else.

As a child I knew who was sick, who was going to die, and who was on the phone before anyone picked it up. When I would tell my parents what I knew, I would always be punished, both verbally and physically. The more I was punished, the madder I got, because my predictions were right most of the time.

One day I commented that one of my father's friends was going to die soon.

"Why do you say that?" my mother asked.

"Because the light around him doesn't stand out very far from his body, and it is very dull," I said.

My father heard me and went into a rage. "Why do you

say things like that?" he cried. "People do not have lights around them! If you don't stop making up things like this, we are going to have to punish you until you learn the difference between make-believe and the real world."

"But the lights are there," I insisted stubbornly.

"No, they are not," he said, then he turned to my mother. "You know, I think it is time we find some outside help for his problem."

My mother said nothing.

"Maybe we should talk to Father Raymond about this," my father suggested.

My mother nodded. "Whatever you think," she said at last.

The following Sunday my parents went to talk to Father Raymond. He agreed to see me during the coming week.

Although my parents were Italian Catholics, we lived in a mostly Polish parish, so that's where we went to Mass. It was also where I was sent to school. My English was broken because I was subjected to too many languages. My parents, being Italian immigrants, spoke only Italian at home, and most of the kids I went to school with spoke Polish. Prayers in school were also in Polish, and I was always forgetting the words or mispronouncing them. The sisters, frustrated by my problems with the language, would punish me severely for this. They'd swat me with a yardstick with such force that the stick would break. After several broken sticks, they decided to try a twelve-inch ruler. Success—this time it didn't break. However, the daily licking made me stand out like a sore thumb and Father Raymond knew me well.

On the appointed day we went to his office, where my father explained to Father Raymond that I insisted I could see various colors of light around people.

"Not only that, but he took hold of a man's wounded hand last week and stopped the bleeding," my father told the priest.

Father Raymond looked grave. "Well, I will pray for your son and anoint him with some holy oil."

I was told to sit in a chair in front of Father Raymond. He opened a large book and started reading a lengthy prayer. After a few minutes my attention span was exhausted and I became fidgety. This earned me some frowns and stern looks from my parents, so I decided I had better try to sit still. Finally Father Raymond finished reading and instructed his housekeeper to bring the holy oil. He dipped his hands into it and administered it to my forehead. He then told my parents he was finished and they could take me home.

Of course, this ritual did not affect my abilities, and I continued to see multicolored rings of light around people.

One day the phone rang and I called out, "That's Aunt Tessie."

"Nonsense," my father exclaimed, "you don't know who's on the other end of the phone."

"Yes I do, it's Aunt Tessie."

My father picked up the phone, and sure enough it was Aunt Tessie.

My father was dumbfounded. After he hung up the phone he said to my mother, "We must take him back to the priest."

Next week we were back in Father Raymond's office. "This time we will do an exorcism," the priest said.

He sat me in the chair again, told his housekeeper to restrain me, and began to pray. I was beginning to thoroughly enjoy all the attention I was getting and I thought it was a great game they were playing with me. I saw that the grown-ups were very serious about all this, but I didn't understand what the consequences would be for me if they didn't get the results they were expecting. Father Raymond read several prayers over me from a large book that was not the Bible. Then he held the cross in front of me and kissed it. He denounced Lucifer, anointed my head with oil, and put a rosary in my hand. He waited for something to happen, but nothing did, so he told my parents to take me home.

After we got home my parents told me to go to my room and think about what had happened. I obliged, but didn't understand what there was to think about.

I was surprised to learn that others couldn't see the lights and the multiple colors I saw around people. I assumed that because *I* could see these colors, everyone else could also. It seemed perfectly natural to me, and since I hadn't learned the art of deception, I continued to blurt out what I observed from time to time. This earned me another trip back to the priest.

"I'm afraid your son has received 'special powers' passed down from Satan," Father Raymond told my father gravely, "but because he is so young, there may be a way to rid him of this evil and save his soul. Make no mistake, this is a very serious situation. But before I do anything more, I suggest you take him to a medical doctor to see if there can be a physical reason for his condition."

So off I went to a medical doctor. I had a checkup and the doctor informed my parents that I was in perfect health.

My parents again consulted the priest. "Well, since I cannot do anything for him, I suggest you take him to a psychiatrist," Father Raymond said.

My parents wanted to do everything they could to ensure that my "evil powers" would not increase, so they dragged me to several psychiatrists. All were baffled by my story and had no solutions to offer.

Perplexed, they ran back to Father Raymond with all the baffling diagnoses by all the doctors.

The priest suggested yet another psychiatrist. Now, you must remember that these events were happening in the 1930s, and the ideas people embraced at the time were more conservative than those held today.

The psychiatrist Father Raymond recommended listened

to my father very carefully as he described the details of my story.

"Well, I think I might be able to help your son," he said. "I think you should consider putting him in a mental institution."

"A mental institution!" my father echoed. "But why? He is not crazy."

"Well, that's debatable," the psychiatrist answered. "He's having delusions, and I think shock treatments might jerk him out of this problem. And, from a religious standpoint, it just might exorcise Satan's hold on him. The devil might not enjoy the unpleasant sensation of the treatments and decide to leave your son's body."

My parents wanted what was best for me, and they had great faith in medical doctors.

"We love you very much," my mother told me that night, "and we want you to have a life free of Satan's hold. If Father Raymond agrees with the psychiatrist, I think we should try it."

Not knowing what kind of situation I was getting into, I passively went along with my parents' decision. The idea of not having to attend school for a while was a mild relief because my classmates either shunned me or teased and taunted me. I'd made the mistake of talking to them about the light around people, so the word was out that I was a weirdo and school became a lonely experience for me. Besides, I really didn't like studying all that much.

I shivered suddenly as I remembered the events of my eighth year. My parents had taken the advice of the psychiatrist and, out of love, sent me to a mental institution instead of the third grade.

"This is for your own good," my father told me. "If we don't do what we can to stop Satan now, you'll become progressively more evil as you grow older."

"Yes, and when you die, Satan will be waiting for you and you'll be punished forever," my mother said.

I didn't like being punished, so the idea that Satan would be waiting to punish me forever was totally unappealing.

"You don't want to grow up to be mean and evil, do you?"

"No," I said. I didn't really understand what it meant to be mean and evil, but I sensed my parents thought it was the worst thing that could happen to me, that it must be something absolutely awful. It never occurred to me that the torture awaiting me would be far worse than anything my parents had ever contemplated.

I remembered that gray morning when we boarded a bus for upstate New York. After driving for two or three hours, we entered a fenced-in area and drove up a winding road until we reached a large brick building. On each side of this large building was a row of two-story buildings with bars on the windows. My parents took me by the hand and led me directly to the reception area where they signed some papers.

The receptionist got on the phone and talked to someone. Pretty soon a man in a white coat appeared at the doorway. He was grossly overweight, his clothes reeked of body odor, and he needed a shave. I stared up at the man, then turned back and looked at my parents. They motioned for me to follow him. I turned just as he stepped forward, grabbed me by the shoulder, and pulled me out of the room.

I didn't have good feelings about this man, and apparently he sensed it, for he had a viselike grip on me as he shoved me toward a large steel door, then took a huge key ring off his belt. While still holding on to my shoulder, he unlocked the door, pushed me inside, and walked me down a long corridor. There were all these doors with little doors built in at an adult's eye level. I had never seen anything like this before. I couldn't imagine why there were little doors on big doors, but I soon found out. These were peepholes used by the attendants to watch the patients.

Finally, after several twists and turns, we reached a small room with nothing but four cots in it. He pushed me in and closed the door behind him.

"Take off all your clothes," he said harshly.

I stared at him with disbelief. I was away from my family for the first time in unfamiliar and unfriendly surroundings. He was a stranger and I really didn't want to undress in front of him, but I knew there would be trouble if I didn't. He searched each article of clothing I took off and then he brought me a uniform that looked somewhat like pajamas. My civilian clothes disappeared and I never saw them again.

I could sense that this man's heart lacked love and compassion, but I wasn't frightened of him. I just didn't enjoy being in his presence. I quickly slipped into the uniform he gave me, then a pair of house slippers, and followed him to a large room that looked like a gymnasium. There were many people milling around. Some were pacing, some playing checkers; some sat in corners rocking, and some screamed their heads off. No one paid any attention to them and they weren't paying any attention to each other. I became very frightened. My instincts told me I was safe and protected, but I was still very scared.

That evening on the cafeteria line, I noticed that you got food only if the people doing the serving liked you; otherwise you were ignored and got nothing. There was nothing that could be done. No one cared.

I didn't have long to ponder the situation I was in, for the next morning an attendant came for me and told me I was to receive my first shock treatment.

I shivered again as I remembered being taken from that warm bed to the cold, wet, stark white room where the attendant prepared me for the shock treatment.

"You are to come with me now," said the attendant.

"Where are we going?" I asked.

"You'll see," he said.

I had no idea what a shock treatment was, and I obediently followed him down a long hall. After making a few turns we entered a small room.

"Okay, take off your clothes."

I obeyed. I was standing there stark naked, feeling very vulnerable and embarrassed. I realized that my rights as a human being to be treated with consideration and respect were being stripped from me. I was powerless to do anything about this unpleasant situation. I knew I was at the mercy of these people and whatever humanity, if any, they might have. They could say and do anything they wanted with me. Fear paralyzed my young body as the attendant entered the room, carrying a cold wet sheet. My survival instincts told me to run, but there was no place to go.

"Okay, let's get up here," he said, pointing to a table that had just been hosed down.

I tried to move, but my feet were glued to the floor. The attendant grabbed my arm roughly and hoisted me up on the table. He then quickly twirled the wet icy sheet around me.

I gasped. The sudden change in temperature took my breath away and left me shaking, shivering, and choking for air. The shock caused me to urinate involuntarily, and this, of course, caused more trouble. The attendant picked up a large pan of ice water and doused me with it. The table had sides with a few holes that allowed the cold water and urine to drain down to the floor.

"How do you like that?"

I couldn't respond. The shock of the experience had numbed me.

How in the name of love could my parents allow this to happen to me? I thought. Then I remembered what Father Raymond had said about Satan not liking this experience. "Well, neither do I," I mumbled quietly to myself.

But as cruel and as inhumane as this experience seemed, it was just a prelude to what was to happen in the next room.

After I stopped gasping for breath, the attendant slid me onto a gurney. He put my arms and legs in leather straps and put another around the middle of my body.

"Why are you strapping me to this table?" I asked in a small voice.

"So you can't get off," he said.

"Why would I want to get off?"

"You'll see," he said, and with that he started wheeling me down the hall to another little room.

"This sheet is cold."

"I know," he said. "It's supposed to be cold."

"But it hurts. I would like to have my clothes back now."

"Not yet. We're not finished with you, my lad."

We entered another room. I was still shivering from the ice-soaked sheets I was wrapped in. A nurse came in and told me to open my mouth. She quickly put a bar into it and strapped it around my head so I couldn't spit it out. I momentarily panicked; I thought I was going to gag and choke to death, but no attempt was made to help me. My chest was heaving, but because of the bar in my mouth I couldn't cough.

"Now, don't you go giving us any trouble," the nurse said. "You might as well make up your mind to put up with this." By way of an explanation she said, "If we didn't put the bar in your mouth, you'd swallow your tongue and choke to death when the electric shock treatment starts."

Swallow my tongue? I thought to myself. How could I possibly do that when I am already choking on whatever it is you have put in my mouth?

"Are you ready?" the attendant asked the nurse. She nodded.

"Okay, everyone stand clear." With that I felt an electric shock shoot through my body. The pain was excruciating, but I couldn't move to get away from it, nor could I protest, as my mouth was gagged.

The electric shock was amplified by the wet sheet wrapped around me. They continued to send what seemed to me life-threatening volts of electricity through my body, until I either went into convulsions or lapsed into unconsciousness. Then they stopped.

I woke up hours later. I was shaking so badly that I had to lock my feet around the foot of the cot to stay on it. I remembered lying on my cot staring into space, totally incapable of moving. I could see people coming into my room and taking my things, but there was nothing I could do. In the numb, paralyzed condition I was in, I couldn't even cry out.

Some inmates would make a practice of keeping track of who went into shock treatments. When the patients were returned to their room in a "vegetable state," the inmates would rush in and steal whatever they could.

The violent impact and pain of the shock treatments affected my ability to remember, not to mention the damage it did to my subtle body and its healing abilities.

Each time I was returned to my room I prayed quietly, "Please God, let me die, so I won't have to continue with these torturous treatments." My prayers weren't answered and the treatments went on and on, for approximately one year.

I remembered the continuous fear I lived with. I never knew when I'd be taken from my warm bed and wrapped in those icy sheets. I called them "installment-plan torture." There was no regular schedule for these dreaded episodes and I sometimes went through one in the morning and another in the evening. But no matter how often or how many treatments I received, there was no way of building up a tolerance to them. Each time I received an electric shock treatment, it was like starting my life all over again because my memory was erased, over and over and over again.

Once a week I would be taken into a room where there were several doctors and they would talk to me and ask me questions I didn't understand.

One doctor would always say, "Now Eugene, tell us your father's name."

"John," I would reply.

"Good, and what does your father do?"

"He is a house painter," I would respond.

These questions would go on for the better part of three-quarters of an hour and then I'd be sent back to my room.

My parents never suspected the kind of treatment I was getting because the institution always made sure I was up and seemingly conscious when they came to visit me. I didn't know how to tell them what I was being put through.

As time went on, I learned that if I played sick long enough, I could miss some of the shock treatments. My survival instincts had been left intact and I was trying to preserve myself and my sanity.

The institution was overcrowded and I got two room-mates. They were two African-American teenagers, Gary and Tom, and they took me under their wings and tried to protect me. They weren't scheduled to receive shock treatments, but they saw what these treatments did to me. I could always see compassion and concern in their eyes when the attendants came for me. They always guarded my things after these episodes, so my belongings stopped disappearing.

One night in the cafeteria, someone came up and took food off my plate. Gary and Tom jumped up, took hold of this guy, and made him return my food. As time passed I felt a great kinship with them; they gave me the feeling that someone there actually cared about what happened to me.

I witnessed many horrors during my time in this institution, and fortunately most of them are now blocked out of

my consciousness. Even though I learned to have little conversation, I was still able to make many friends there.
Looking back, I now think the purpose for my being put into
the hospital was to continue my healing work. Whether
unconsciously or consciously, everyone there had problems.
They all needed help and understanding, and I felt that,
somehow, I was helping.

This place was not segregated by age or sex. Everyone
was thrown together, and the horrors of insanity prevailed
on every level imaginable.

One lesson I learned very quickly was to never, ever discuss my insights about forthcoming events or the auras I
saw around people, especially with adults. If I mentioned to
the adults there the fact that someone had a weak life force,
I was immediately taken for another shock treatment.

By the end of a year I had stopped talking about what I
saw, and my parents were notified that they could take me
home.

I remember the attendant coming into my room one day,
and I braced myself, thinking I was going to be taken for
another treatment. Instead, he announced, "The doctors
have decided you're well now. You're going home."

I smiled but said nothing. By this time I had endured so
much excruciating pain that I was emotionally numb. I was
on "automatic." I had no happy or unhappy moments. Most
of the time I felt nothing and tried to avoid adults at all costs.

Later that day my parents came to take me home. I was
very quiet and withdrawn after this experience. I spent as
much time as I could alone in my room after that year and
never talked to anyone unless I was asked a direct question.

My intuitive abilities were very badly damaged but, with
the passing of time, they began coming back. I could see
auras around people again but knew better than to tell anyone. I slept a lot and avoided people.

❖   ❖   ❖

Now, as I stared out of my bedroom window at the Leningrad sky, I looked at my watch and realized how late it was. The night sky was still bright but I still wasn't sleepy, and I couldn't stop the flood of memories. My thoughts shifted back to the time when I was in the hospital after my operation.

It was the day after my first operation. I awoke and my first impulse was to get out of bed. I started to move and a blond, very beautiful woman in white came forward and touched me very gently on the arm indicating that I wasn't to get out of bed. She had a tender smile, and when I looked into her eyes I felt her warmth and loving compassion.

I didn't know how to respond to those emotions, as I had rarely experienced such gentleness or kindness from anyone and wondered how long it would be before she scolded me. Wasn't she an adult and didn't adults always scold? I regarded her passively.

"How are you?" she asked, with a smile.

"Okay, I guess."

"My name is Nancy, I'm your nurse. I'll be looking in on you every day," she said. "Is there anything I can get you?"

"No," I answered.

When she made her rounds, she'd sit with me for a while and read. I'd never known anyone like her and I became very attached to her. Nancy's gentleness was like an elixir and my health began to improve rapidly. The pain had stopped, but the tube was still inserted in my side. Four mornings later, I woke up hot and very dizzy, and the pain had started up again.

"I feel very hot and my side hurts," I told Nancy when she came in to see me that morning.

"I'll get the doctor immediately," she answered, and went hurrying out of the room.

The doctor, however, ignored her. The pain became so excruciating that I couldn't move. The only way I had some relief was if I lay flat on my back. If I made the slightest turn it became unbearable. I could see the clock fading in and out and the curtains around the bed were changing colors. I endured the pain as long as I could and then nature intervened and I lapsed into a state of unconsciousness.

When help finally came, it was obvious I was in need of immediate attention, and I was quickly wheeled into the brightly lit room to be operated on a second time. I had developed a severe case of peritonitis; every drop of blood in my body was poisoned. By the time they got me into the operating room I was already leaving my body; I knew it because there I was, up on the ceiling again.

Oh boy, here I go again. I'm getting a second chance, and this time I'm going to stay! I thought to myself.

As I was whisked up into the dark tunnel, I recognized, once again, the collage of colors and the sensation of going toward the light. The light beings motioned me to follow. I felt the exhilaration of being where I wanted to be, but again I was being sent back.

The return was like a movie running in reverse, and suddenly, thud! I was back in my body. These two experiences, in a matter of four days, did not change me or my outlook on life, but rather affirmed what I had instinctively known as a five-year-old: Basically, there is something to look forward to after we finish our lessons on this school called Earth. Our souls have chosen to be in a body to have the physical experiences necessary to evolve, so we had better get on with it.

After this second close call the doctors were more attentive to my healing process. Three months later I was allowed to go home, but the doctors said that I'd always be frail and weak.

The upside of this was that my parents gave me more love and care than before. Because of my condition, I was closely watched and not allowed to leave the house, except to go to school.

As time passed, I grew stronger and the little boy in me became interested in baseball. I would watch the kids playing at recess and I wanted to play too, despite all the warnings. I obtained a baseball glove and began practicing in out-of-the-way places where no one who knew me would see me. I couldn't take the baseball glove into the house for fear of my parents finding it, so I hid it under our front porch. My practice finally paid off — I got good enough that the guys let me play with them, and I would sneak out of the house to play.

This went on for about a year. One night, however, my parents saw me put something under the porch, and my father found the glove. He came inside and held it up to show my mother. "What are you doing with this?" he asked, without raising his voice.

"Playing baseball," I said.

"The doctors said you could never play sports. It's too dangerous," he said sternly.

"Well, I feel okay, and besides, I'm careful," I said.

"How long have you been doing this?" Mother asked.

"About a year."

"You know you are flirting with death," she said. "Do you want to die?"

"No, I just want to play baseball," I said, with the wide-eyed conviction of a child.

She shook her head and looked helplessly at my father. I could hear the concern in her voice, but instead of instilling caution in me, it made me want to play baseball even more, and there was nothing anyone could say to me that could dampen my enthusiasm for the sport.

"Please let me play," I begged. "I'm good, and the kids want me to play with them."

"This means a lot to you, doesn't it?" my mother asked.

"Yes, it does," I said.

"Your mother and I will think about it," my father said, "but until we decide you're grounded."

I was grounded for a year, but I continued to grow stronger and my parents finally gave in.

My folks approved of baseball, because it was a normal, American boy's thing. They believed I had truly left my old ways behind, and I never, ever displayed any inclination toward the healing abilities that I still had. As far as my parents were concerned, the treatments had paid off; I behaved in the way they expected, ignored all my intuitive abilities, and continued on the road to "normalcy."

During my high school years I became good enough at baseball to be asked to play on an amateur team that was sponsored by a private men's club. This was a great honor and so much fun that I entertained the idea of trying to play professional ball when I got out of high school.

Unconsciously I was determined to become "normal," to do everything the average guy would do. No matter what happened to my natural self, I was going to conform. During the Korean War I volunteered for the navy. After the war I married my best friend's sister, Karen. I moved to California, and had the kids, the house—the whole business. I now had the whole American Enchilada.

I was determined to fit in: I wouldn't believe in anything I couldn't see. If I couldn't touch it, it wasn't real, and therefore didn't exist. I was fully accepted by my peers; I was one of the "boys." I was Mr. Normal.

Little did I know what lay ahead of me, how many years would go by and what I would have to go through to return to that special place that had been so natural for me as a child.

My Path Home

I knew I needed to sleep, but the light was having a strange effect on me, and I was asking myself, Why, why here in Leningrad, of all places, am I reliving so much of my past? I lay down on the bed, got up, impatiently walked around the room, sat in a high-backed chair, and then pulled it toward the open window and stared out onto the city. Perhaps it was the wonderful play of light in the night sky that resembled the lights of my past, or perhaps it was the incredible energy I felt that afternoon at the cemetery. I didn't know and I truly didn't care. I was exhilarated because I was feeling the pain of my past and knew that I was being healed.

I remembered the patriotism I'd felt when I left high school for the navy. I wasn't old enough to join, but I was big, and with a little finagling, I convinced the people in charge that I was old enough to defend my country. The tremendous wave of pride I felt when I was notified that I was to show up for basic training is still clear in my memory. On a personal level, I wanted to travel and see the world, but my primary goal was to go and fight for my country. The universe, however, had other plans for me. I went everywhere *but* Korea. I did my basic training in Norfolk, Virginia; then I was stationed in the Bahamas; finally, I was sent to Iceland. Although the discipline was rigid, I enjoyed life in the navy.

I had a lot of fun, made some good friends, and was trained in electrical work. I briefly considered the navy as a career, but when my stint was up I decided to come home. My parents still lived in Yonkers, and I knew my old room would be waiting for me. Unlike today, it was acceptable then for children to live with their parents until they started their own home, so I didn't have the hassle of finding a place to live when I got back to Yonkers.

I was still in my teens when I was discharged, so my main interests were sports, cars, and girls. Like every teenager, I desperately wanted a new car, but before I could buy one I needed a job. This was the 1950s and America's economy was still expanding, so finding a job was no problem. I got the first one I applied for.

I was now a construction worker on the Tappan Zee Bridge. As I looked back on this experience, I realized that this was a very dangerous job, but at the time I was young and never noticed the danger. The only thing on my mind was the paycheck at the end of the week, which brought me closer to my dream automobile. It was easy for a hardworking kid, and soon I had enough money to buy the car. After looking at several, I decided on a Mercury. I drove it home, pulled up in front of my parents', and felt great. This son of Italian immigrants could afford a new car! My parents were proud too, and this made me very happy.

The construction work I was doing on the bridge was physically demanding, and I wasn't aware of the muscles I was building until the night I got in my Mercury and took hold of the steering wheel with such force it broke in two. I was astounded—that wasn't the image I had of myself—and I decided right then and there that I was getting too muscular, too strong, and I drove off with the broken steering wheel and never returned to the Tappan Zee Bridge.

As luck would have it, I got a job almost immediately with a utility company. There I was able to use the electrical training I had received in the navy, and there was room for advancement. I felt pretty good about this, and as I had more than enough money, I started dating my friend's sister, Karen.

She was young and beautiful and fun, and after dating for about a year, I decided it was time to get married. My parents said I could take the bottom apartment of their house to start housekeeping, and they'd move upstairs to the apartment where Joseph had lived.

After the wedding, Mr. and Mrs. Normal headed off for the traditional honeymoon trip to Niagara Falls.

When we returned, the apartment was waiting for us. Everything was falling into place. I was living the life of Mr. Average American Householder, and it felt right. I'd succeeded in neatly sweeping my old ways under the carpet and convinced myself they no longer existed. I'd gotten a couple of promotions and was well on my way to having a piece of the American Dream.

A year later we became parents to a beautiful little girl, whom we named Diane. I was a proud father, progressive for those days, and I made an attempt at sharing the parenting. One day when Karen went shopping, I offered to take care of Diane. Feeding time came and I fed her a jar of applesauce. She finished it in no time flat and indicated that she wanted another. Being the good family provider, I gave her another and another. Five jars later we were in the bathroom for a considerable length of time. When my wife got home, she was not happy about my generous feeding spree, and I was forever grounded from babysitting.

I continued to get promotions on my job and finally we were able to buy a large house in Upper Westchester County. By this time we had two more daughters, Annie and Vickie, and a son, John, whom we named after my father. Everything was going well. I had a good job, a happy, healthy family, and I was able to provide all the material things my family and I needed. This lifestyle continued for two and a half decades. By all outward appearances I had made the adjustment to "normal." No one, not even my wife, knew about my childhood.

By ignoring and denying my natural abilities, I had convinced myself that they'd gone away and the life I was living was as it should be. From time to time I would have flashes of insight about forthcoming events. More often than not the events would turn out exactly as I had foreseen, but I never put two and two together, or realized that I could witness events outside of time, or that my rate of accuracy was too high to dismiss as coincidence or the law of averages. Instead, I continued to ignore these happenings to the point of denying that I had ever had the insights in the first place.

That "normal family lifestyle" was not to continue much longer for me. By the 1970s, this American life was beginning to fall into decadence. Job salaries were going down and taxes were going up, especially in New York. It was becoming increasingly difficult for me to maintain a decent way of life for me and my family. I was becoming more and more disgusted with the growing crime rate and the pollution. I didn't want my children growing up in this environment. The straw that broke the camel's back was an increase in my real estate taxes. That did it, I thought, I was moving all of us to the West Coast, where it was still possible to maintain a decent way of life.

I had enjoyed my work with the utility company, having moved up to middle management, with pensions and health benefits and a company car, but it was time for me to have my own business. I knew if I cashed in my company pension, I would have the funds necessary to buy a business in California. As luck would have it I found an electrical contractor who wanted to retire, and I bought him out. Part of the agreement was that he would stay on for a year to help me familiarize myself with the business. I now had my own business, and I was ready to move.

By this time, my two oldest daughters were married, but they too decided they wanted to move to California. They gathered up their belongings and we all headed west in our respective campers. It was quite an adventure. After several cross-country mishaps and a considerable amount of back-tracking to find one another when we got separated, we finally arrived in California.

My wife and I found a home in the San Diego area. It was a pleasant yet sad house. When I bought it, I didn't know anything about numerology or its effect on the house address; ours was 5555. The number 5 in numerology implies a life filled with change and new experiences, so I guess I had it coming to me. In essence those four 5s changed every aspect of my life.

We had barely moved west when my home life started becoming rocky. I wasn't worried, for I thought it was a phase we were going through. With the passing of time everything would smooth itself out, I thought, and things would get back to normal. I thought wrong!

Sitting at the breakfast table one morning, Karen looked at me and said, "I've decided to file for divorce. I found a lawyer yesterday and I've started the proceedings."

I was stunned. "What!" I exclaimed. It was completely unexpected. We'd never even discussed the possibility of parting, and here she was telling me about lawyers, and ending a marriage of twenty-five years.

"I don't want to stay in this house," she continued. "I'd like to sell my part to you and move into an apartment."

"Whatever you want," I said, too numb to say anything else.

She left shortly after that and I was completely alone for the first time in my life. I still had my electrical contracting business, and I threw myself into it, allowing it to completely absorb my life. That nagging feeling of not being where I should be was beginning to surface more often now and for longer periods of time, but I still continued to work at the only profession I knew.

Time went by, and little things started to tell me that I wasn't where I should be. I couldn't exactly put my finger on what was happening, so I continued to ignore these annoying and perplexing warnings. I held out until the universe gave me a wake-up call that was impossible to ignore.

I woke up early one Monday morning with the uncomfortable feeling of impending disaster, but I chose to ignore it. It turned out to be the day I received notice that my divorce was final. I was no longer married. I read the notice with a sinking heart. A feeling of emptiness and loss filled my being.

How could something that started out so well have such an unhappy ending? I spent the evening reflecting on this situation. It was impossible to sleep; the feeling of something being terribly wrong stayed with me throughout the night.

The next morning I got ready to go to work, thankful that I had a job to go to and something to think about that would take my mind off my problems. I got to work early. Nine o'clock came and went and my partner didn't show up. I didn't think much about it, but as the morning wore on and I didn't hear from him, I became concerned and decided to call his home.

The phone rang once and a recording came on. "The number you have dialed, 555-5555, has been disconnected."

"How odd," I mumbled. I called the operator and told her what had happened.

She checked and said, "That number was disconnected yesterday."

What could have happened? I thought to myself, Our business is doing well, and I'm sure he's not having any financial difficulties.

After calling several of his friends and discovering that none of them knew his whereabouts, the realization began to sink in slowly that he had left town in a hurry. This point became crystal clear to me when a supplier called later in the day.

"You know, the check you wrote me bounced," he said, annoyance in his voice. "I'm sure there's some misunderstanding at the bank, but I'd appreciate it if you'd get it straightened out."

"Sure, I'll call the bank immediately and take care of it," I assured him.

I telephoned the bank and got a clerk. I identified myself and my account number. "A check I wrote to one of my suppliers bounced," I told the clerk. "How could that happen? I know there are sufficient funds in the account to cover the check."

"I'll look it up." A couple of minutes passed. Finally he came back on the phone: "Ah, here it is. Well, the reason the check bounced is that the account no longer exists."

"What!" I exclaimed.

"Our records show that all the funds were withdrawn yesterday and the account was closed."

"Thank you for your trouble."

I knew my partner had a cabin in the mountains, so I got in my car and drove up there, only to discover that he had sold the place.

"We bought the cabin from him last month," the new owners said.

"Well, did he say where he was going?"

"No, he just said he was tired of the responsibility of taking care of the cabin and wanted to get rid of it, so he could have more free time."

I drove home in a state of dazed disbelief. My partner had taken the company's entire liquid assets and left the state without a trace. My company was bankrupt.

I spent another sleepless night realizing that I couldn't even meet the week's payroll without withdrawing money from my personal savings account, which was already anemic after having paid my wife for her half of our home. I was going to meet the payroll, regardless of the personal hardship it created. On Wednesday morning I went to the bank, withdrew my entire savings account, and headed out to pay the workers and tell them that I could no longer afford to have anyone working for me.

What started out as a solemn day turned into a nightmare. As I drove to the job site, an out-of-control speeding car spun across the middle divider and hit me head-on. There was nothing I could do. I'd lost control, and I was once again at the mercy of outside forces. The car slid off the road and came to a halt on a steep embankment. Although greatly shaken, I had enough survival instinct to get the door open and get out of the car. I had just fueled up, and the terrific impact of the collision caused gas to spill all over the highway, an impending invitation for an infernal explosion.

The fire department arrived within minutes of the crash and was followed by the police and medics. I was standing on the side of the road with a few scratches on my face and a tingle in my left side. As I stood there I realized that my entire life savings was in an attaché case in the trunk of my automobile. I had blindly started for it when a fireman came running over and grabbed me.

"Where do you think you're going?" he said sharply.

"To get my attaché case out of my trunk," I answered calmly.

"Oh, no you're not," he said. "That car could explode at any moment."

"Yes, I know, and it won't matter after I get my attaché case."

The fireman grabbed me again. As he pulled, I realized I was badly hurt because the pain that shot through my rib cage was razor sharp. All my determination and physical strength went into one quick jerk — I was free of the fireman and headed for my car.

I knew I was taking a tremendous risk — almost anything could cause the whole area to go up in flames — but I had to have that attaché case. I wanted the men who had stood by me to be paid for their work.

I got the case and got back without a mishap. By this time the ambulance had arrived, and a policeman stormed up to me. "Get into the ambulance, we're going to take you to the local hospital."

I knew I had to go to a hospital, but I had a bad feeling about this one in particular. "No, I'm not getting into that ambulance. I want to go to the hospital in Palm Springs."

"This ambulance doesn't go that far."

"I know," I said, "that's why I'm not getting into it."

"You have to go," the policeman said. "You need immediate attention. There's no way to know what may have happened to you in that crash."

"I know," I replied, "and I will. If you'll let me call my secretary, she'll get me to the hospital in Palm Springs."

Reluctantly he let me go. I went to the phone and called my secretary. "I have a small problem with my car," I said, "and I need you to pick me up."

"I'll be there in twenty minutes," she said.

"I'll be here."

When she arrived my car was being towed and I was sitting on top of my attaché case. One glance at me and she exclaimed, "Oh my, oh my, oh my! Why didn't you tell me you were in an accident? Are you hurt?"

"I think I may have broken some ribs. Would you take me to the hospital in Palm Springs?"

"I'll have you there in no time," she said.

"Now, I don't want to waste much time in that hospital," I told her. "Today is payday, and I have to get to the job site."

"Okay, you're the boss."

The men who worked for me were a special group, who had stuck with me through bad times, and I wanted to see them get a decent send-off.

The emergency room was like a scene out of a Laurel and Hardy movie. I was given a cup and told to go to the bathroom and fill it. I was too excited to be able to comply and came out of the bathroom with an empty cup. Out of the corner of my eye I saw a full specimen sitting on a table and I took it. It turned out the specimen I'd taken belonged to a pregnant woman.

When I later realized what I had done I chuckled. The results probably gave some lab technician an interesting, if not unusual, day.

Next, a lady walked up and told me she needed to take blood. I looked at her and sensed her nervousness.

"Is this the first time you're taking blood from someone?" She nodded. "Yes, it is."

"No way," I said. "You go find someone else to practice on, because you're not going to practice on me."

She stormed off and reported to her supervisor. This brought a tough lady out of her office, and I had to endure a rather lengthy lecture about the new technician's qualifications. Finally the situation was resolved.

Then came the X-ray room. The technician there turned out to be from New York, and we started a conversation. Since she wasn't concentrating 100 percent on her work, she accidentally dropped the X-ray plate onto my face, causing me to have a severe nosebleed and a rather deep gash in my forehead.

She was petrified. "Please, please don't tell anyone about this or I'll lose my job."

"Okay," I said, "just give me a bandage for my forehead so the blood doesn't run into my eyes."

She rummaged through several drawers for a couple of

minutes and came up with a patch. "I don't have any bandages, how about a patch?" she said lamely.

"Okay, I guess that'll have to do."

She put the patch on my forehead and I went back to the emergency room. When the doctor came in to tell me I had some fractured ribs, he looked at me and said, "But what happened to your forehead? It looks pretty bad; we better take a look at it."

"Just give me my clothes, and let me out of here before you kill me," I said.

I was leaving in worse shape than when I'd arrived, but I was determined to get through the day. I motioned to my secretary, who gathered up my belongings and drove me to the job site.

I gave each worker his pay, wished him well, and went home. For once I was thankful the day only had twenty-four hours. I needed a rest badly! Not only was I emotionally wiped out, but my physical body was also a wreck and I needed to mend. I figured the worst was over. What else could happen? I found out the next day, a Thursday. That was the day I lost more of my assets at the job site.

On Friday, the general contractor I was working for in Palm Springs threw me off the job and put a fence around my equipment and materials. In essence, this guy legally stole everything my business had. Since my equipment was sitting on government property it would be a federal offense if I moved the stuff off the grounds.

In less than a week the entire structure of my life had collapsed. I was helpless. I had no one to turn to and didn't know what direction to follow. I was glad I had the weekend—I needed the time to rest and recuperate.

I came home, sat in my favorite chair, and watched television for two days.

Monday morning rolled around, and I decided that my first priority was finding work. I held an electrical contractor's license, I had many years of experience, and I didn't think finding immediate work would be a problem. Boy, was I wrong. The fact that I had owned a business scared off several potential bosses. "Why are you here when you have had such extensive experience?" "You're overqualified." "You're too old." "You're underqualified."

This went on for a week. Every attempt I made to get work ended in rejection. I was concerned—bills were coming in and I had no way of meeting them. My material property was slowly being repossessed. My cars were taken from me in the middle of the night. I saved the one I was driving by chaining it to an avocado tree. I couldn't meet the payments on the house, it went into foreclosure, and I still couldn't find work.

Finally, in the middle of the second week, I landed a small contracting job. It paid just enough to buy groceries and gas for the week. I figured this job would eventually lead to something more substantial, but it didn't. The universe was challenging me, giving me just enough to survive and nothing more. The situation wasn't good, but I was stubborn enough to believe it was just temporary, and things would be the way they used to be.

Three months passed and I was forced to sell my gold watch. I became emotionally numb and wasn't thinking much about the future.

My kids were really wonderful at this time. They were constantly calling and encouraging me: I would find a job, I just had to have faith and give it time. Deep down I wanted to agree with them, but the reality of the moment was tough to face.

I didn't think anything else could possibly happen, as there was nothing left. I was in a state of despair, and I had momentary flashes of being out of control. My subconscious knew that a higher force was at work, but in my waking conscious state the stubborn conformist in me thought I would be able to ride out this storm, that I could put it all back together.

On a Saturday morning the phone rang. I jumped to answer it, hoping that it was going to be a job offer. I recognized the voice of a casual acquaintance.

"Gene?"

"Yes," I answered.

"This is Jenny."

I paused, wondering why she was calling me. "Well, how are you?"

"Okay. You know, Gene, I had a dream about you last night and it was so real I would like to come over and talk to you."

"That's really what I need right now, Jenny, a good dream," I replied sarcastically.

She ignored my remark and continued: "I really need to talk to you. Is it okay if I come over for a while?"

"What kind of dream did you have about me?" I asked casually, ignoring her request to come over.

"I dreamed you healed me."

"Healed you?"

"Yes," she said.

All my skepticism from years of denial kicked in. "Have you been taking drugs?" I asked.

"No! No, it's nothing like that. Please, I really need to talk to you. This dream was just so real that I feel I must see you."

Reluctantly, I agreed. "Okay, come on over, but I have to tell you, this dream of yours doesn't make any sense to me."

"I'll be there in about half an hour," she said.

"Wait a minute," I said. "In this dream, what affliction did you have that I healed?"

"Oh, I have a bad case of herpes zoster," she said. "I'll see you in a few minutes." She hung up before I could change my mind about allowing her to come.

I knew that herpes was highly contagious, and my heart sank. It was too late to stop her, so I decided that we would sit at opposite ends of the kitchen table and, hopefully, I'd escape this dreadful malady.

I wasn't particularly religious, nor had I ever had any interest in spirituality, so I was rather skeptical about this dream of hers. If she wanted to be healed, why didn't she go to a doctor? I thought to myself. That's what doctors do, not electrical contractors.

Approximately half an hour later the doorbell rang, and there she was. I opened the door to what could have been a very attractive woman in her thirties, but the parts of her body that were not clothed showed multiple herpes blisters. I looked at her and was filled with total compassion for her and her situation. I felt the frustration and anxiety she was feeling.

"Come on in," I said, pulling a chair from the kitchen table for her. "Why don't you sit down and tell me about this dream of yours?"

Instead of sitting on the other side of the table, as I had planned, I found myself sitting next to her.

She looked into my eyes and began crying.

"What's wrong?" I asked.

"Everything we've said and done so far is exactly the way it was in the dream, except you put your hand on my shoulder." With that, she lifted my hand by the wrist and let it rest on her shoulder. Then she closed her eyes and her head fell over toward her chest.

I looked at her. "What's wrong?" I asked again.

There was no response.

"Are you okay?" Again, no response.

This is silly, I thought to myself. Why am I sitting here with my hand on her shoulder while she's asleep?

I didn't know what to do, so I sat there for a few more minutes, and then Mr. Normal kicked in and again I thought, This is ridiculous, why am I here? What am I doing? I started to remove my hand but discovered, much to my surprise, that it wouldn't move. A force seemed to have my hand glued to her shoulder.

I waited another few minutes and tried again. This time I was determined to pull my hand away, and I used more force, but it still didn't budge. I actually lifted her off the chair she was sitting on, but my hand held tightly to her shoulder. I sat there trying to figure out what was going on.

About twenty minutes went by, then her head came up, her eyes fluttered open, my hand came off her shoulder, and she smiled.

"Gene, I feel pretty good now," she said.

I looked at her. "Well, I'm glad."

"I have to go now. Thank you for letting me come over."

"Any time," I answered.

With that she was up and out the door.

What a flake, I thought to myself after she had left. Imagine thinking that by putting my hand on her shoulder all those blisters would disappear! I then remembered that I had touched the blisters. I washed my hands for several minutes, dismissed the issue from my mind, and decided to watch some television.

The doorbell rang again. I wasn't expecting anyone, but judging from the way things were going, I was afraid the men in the white coats were coming to get me.

I said to myself, They won't need a straightjacket: I'll go willingly. Who knows? Maybe after a long rest and some help I'll be okay.

But when I opened the door, it was only a uniformed man coming to shut my water off. He was a nice guy, sympathetic to my situation, and suggested I fill the bathtub before he turned the water off. After his task was finished, I went back to my chair determined to watch some TV. I sat down and was just getting comfortable when the doorbell rang again.

This time it was the electric company, who came to cut the power. They did what they had to do and left. Now I couldn't even watch television, but I still had my old, favorite chair. I sat down, trying to make some sense out of the day.

The next morning the phone rang, and when I picked it up I heard Jenny speaking very loudly and excitedly.

"Calm down," I said, "and speak so I can understand you. Now, what are you trying to tell me?"

"You won't believe it, but when I woke up this morning, there wasn't a blister anywhere on my body. It's just like the dream. Can I come over and show you?"

"Sure. Why not?" I said.

I later opened the door to a radiantly happy woman. There wasn't a single blemish on her skin.

"Isn't it great!" she exclaimed.

I was taken aback and totally speechless, as I gazed at this attractive woman who was the picture of perfect health.

"How could this be?" I mumbled, then my other self kicked in and I heard myself saying, "Go to your doctor right away and get checked up. Then come back and see me."

"Okay," she said, "but I don't really need a doctor now."

"Go anyway," I commanded.

She left and I stood there very confused and frightened. I was so frightened I locked the garage and every door and window in the house. My rational side was trying to lock out the force that had healed Jenny.

Still very shaken, I sat down and tried to make some sense out of what had happened. It suddenly became clear that I was hallucinating, the stress had cracked me. None of this had happened at all. The whole thing was a mirage; Jenny hadn't been there. I calmed down after a while, but the question kept repeating over and over again: Why healing? Why after all the years of repressing my God-given powers were they again a force in my life?

I know today that Jenny was the catalyst I needed to change my life. I needed to see her in perfect health after my hand had rested on her shoulder. I didn't know it then but that incident set the stage for everything that came later.

As I sat trying to understand, I fell into a deep sleep. I found out later that I never moved from that chair for a period of three days. My children later told me they took turns coming by each day, but I hadn't been aware of it. I know now that I was being worked on by higher powers. The damage that had been done to my intuitive gifts by the electric shock treatments was being repaired, my gift was being fine-tuned, and my mission was being explained to me. Although it would be some time before this healing would make a drastic change in my life, this was indeed the beginning. As I look back on this traumatic time, I find it ironic that as my energy was being turned on everything around me was being turned off.

I woke up not knowing I'd slept so long. I had a funny feeling in my body. I stood up, walked around, and looked out the window at the avocado tree. I could feel it growing, I could feel the roots extending into the ground and the sap flowing up the trunk and out into the leaves. The wind wasn't blowing, but I could feel its presence. I could see the air vibrating in brilliantly colored waves. The universe was teeming with life that I had never noticed before. I got in my car and drove off with only the clothes on my back. I left everything behind, and I never looked back.

My two sisters, who had chosen careers instead of marriage, shared a house. I drove over there, went in, and said, "I need a place to stay."

"Stay as long as you like," Anna Marie said, and Antonette nodded in agreement.

"I've been asleep for three days," I said.

"That seems like a long time to sleep," Anna Marie said calmly.

"Yes," I said. "I don't know what's happening to me. My body feels strange and I can see and feel things I didn't even know existed. On the way over here almost every person I looked at had a halo of brilliant white light extending around their heads and down their shoulders. It was so distracting that I nearly ran a couple of stoplights."

"You used to say things like that when you were a child."

"Yes, I know."

My sisters nodded their heads.

Although I wasn't aware of it, this was the end of the old and the beginning of the new for me. I will always be grateful for my sisters' tolerance, for their unconditional acceptance of me during this fantastic period of transition.

Time passed, and I continued to try and find work as an electrical contractor. I would get little jobs here and there, but nothing substantial. I didn't understand why, but now I knew the universe had no intention of letting me slip back into the comfortable life of householder and businessman. Again the universe was providing for me by allowing me to get just enough work to take care of my basic needs. I lingered in the old ways, but the new was slowly but surely taking hold. I was beginning to be able to accept the loss of my role as head of a household, while the bachelor life I had been plunged into was starting to feel comfortable and at times even enjoyable. I didn't have to pay rent or buy food; my only expense was my car.

One morning, after a short drive to the grocery store, I decided the cooling system in my car needed to be flushed and I went at it. There was a special way to release the pressure on the radiator cap but this time the cap blew off in my hands and a geyser of hot steam came shooting out. It happened so fast I couldn't get my arm out of the way and I burned my right forearm badly. I ran into the house. My sister Anna Marie, a registered nurse with a career in the emergency ward, immediately put salve on it to draw out the heat and then wrapped it.

"You should go to the hospital and let them take a look at that," she said. "It's very serious."

"I'm not going to any hospital."

She didn't answer, but later in the evening she brought it up again.

"Why should I go to the hospital? You've already bandaged it."

"It's a serious burn, and infection could set in," she replied.

I didn't say anything more, but as I sat there trying to decide whether or not to take her advice, I had an insight. If I was running around healing others, maybe I could also heal myself. I decided to give it a try. I casually let my left hand rest over the spot that was burned and left it there through the night.

The next morning when I joined Anna Marie at the breakfast table, she again suggested a visit to the hospital.

"I don't see why I should go to the hospital," I said. "I feel fine and, besides, the pain around the burn area has stopped."

"Well, at least let me change the bandage," she said.

"Okay, take a look. If it's as bad as you think it is, I'll go."

I held out my arm and she started unwrapping the bandage. When she finished, she stepped back and looked puzzled. I followed her eyes to my arm: Only two tiny red spots were visible. I looked up at her and grinned.

"I don't understand how this is possible," she said.

"Well, last night, I decided to do a little experiment," I said. "I thought that since I was calling myself a healer I should see if I could heal myself, so I kept my hand on my arm throughout the evening and into the morning."

She shook her head. "In all my years as a nurse, I've

never seen a burn as serious as this one disappear overnight. I feel like I'm in the Twilight Zone."

We looked at each other and broke out laughing.

By now I had started dating and going to social functions. One night my date Vera and I were invited to a party. We'd been there less than a quarter of an hour when she came to me and told me she had a severe headache. Without thinking, I put my hand on her forehead—an automatic reaction, an affectionate gesture. Within a minute or so, she looked at me incredulously.

"What did you do?" she asked.

"Nothing," I said. "I just touched your head."

"But my headache is completely gone."

To alleviate their pain I'd put my hands on people many times before, but in this instance the gesture hadn't been a conscious attempt to heal. "Well, I'm glad," I said sheepishly. "That means we don't have to go home just yet."

Several people overheard our conversation. One man came over to me and said, "Hey, Gene, I've had this pain in my shoulder for a month. Can you fix that too?"

I put my hand on his shoulder. About ten minutes later he exclaimed, "Hey, it doesn't hurt anymore!"

The next thing I knew I had become the center of attention, and a line of people formed, each with a mild complaint for me to work on. Later that evening Vera asked me if I would work on her aunt.

"My Aunt Millie has cancer and the doctors have told her she won't live."

"Well, I've never worked on anyone with cancer before, but I'll be glad to do what I can," I said.

I later found out that this kind of healing is what's called the "laying on of hands." I would like to point out that I was never interested in school or spent more than a little time on books; all the knowledge I acquired was either from doing or by listening to my inner voice.

I worked on Vera's aunt every day for two weeks, and when she went for her monthly checkup, the doctors could find no cancer or any evidence that there had ever been any cancer. Her current X-rays showed nothing.

This was the test that launched me into healing, although I still didn't want to do it. The "healer" in me was starting to work, but Mr. Normal wasn't accepting him. This was a war that was to go on for a considerable length of time.

I Become a Popular Party Item

We were in the early 1980s now and the word was out that I could make people feel better by laying my hands on them, so I was getting invitations to lots of parties. It seemed everyone had an ailment that needed attention. I worked on a lot of people, and they always felt better.

All this was done intuitively. As I tuned into the person's life force, my hands seemed to know where to go and what to do; it was as if they were guided by some unseen force. My job was to accept this force and trust it, and that wasn't easy for me. I'd always wanted to know why something worked, I needed to see physical proof, and now here it was: People were actually getting healthy under my touch and I was actually beginning to believe it.

Many people spend years studying and practicing before they enter a profession, but that wasn't my experience. All the knowledge I required was suddenly *there*. I know now that it had always been there, and that my childhood traumas blocked it out. Now I was letting the energy flow again, and its powers constantly amazed me. I could see the time line between the ethereal and our earthly dimension. I found that if I needed information, it would come to me simply by meditating on it.

I had the ability to communicate by clairvoyance or clairaudience even with those on the other side of the world. This method of communication was two-way: I was able to send or receive thoughts mentally or audibly with little or no effort. Also, my touch was capable of jump-starting the life force of others. Sometimes the energy that came through me was so strong that my physical body was taxed to its limit. I had to learn how to control the flow, to know when it was necessary to stop it.

I was starting to have fun with this gift. I was truly fascinated by its many facets, but was still doing electrical contracting to pay the bills. My gift had become a hobby I couldn't leave alone. It never occurred to me to charge money for it. After all, it was apparently a gift from God, it wasn't mine. How could *I* charge for it? *God* never charged for anything!

This way of thinking had me working an eighteen-hour day. I would do my electrical contracting morning and afternoon, and in the evenings I would do healings.

One day when I was working on a lady on a park bench, the weather was nippy, and we were uncomfortable. She looked at me and said, "You know, Gene, it's time you got an office. People should come to you, instead of you going to them."

I smiled and said, "Well, that would be nice, but I don't have the money for next month's rent, let alone money for an office."

"I know a lady who has a beautiful house in San Diego, and she rents rooms. Let's give it a shot," she replied.

Before I could say no, we were driving to see it. It was a beautiful house, easily worth $1800 to $2000 a month.

"Look," said the landlady, "I want to rent the whole house to you. You need the space, make me an offer."

I ran my fingers over the $1.75 in my pocket and decided that the only way I was going to get out of there was to make this woman an absurd offer.

"Okay," I said, "I'd be willing to pay $975 a month for this place, but I don't have the money for the deposit or the month's rent in advance."

"Fine," she said. "When do you want to move in?"

I was floored, and hoped she would back out when I stammered, "Well, not immediately," but the lady held me to my word. A deal was a deal and I was stuck with it.

At the time I had a roommate. When I told her about the house she was pleased but, like me, drew a blank on how we would come up with the money. But things were turning around. I was using my gift more and more and, as luck would have it, I got a call from a lady with a bad back problem.

"I have been to doctors all across the United States," Nora told me, "and none of them have been able to help me."

"Well, let's give it a try and see what happens," I told her. "I don't have an office, but there's a church that allows me to use their basement. If you can meet me there at 8 P.M. I'll see what I can do for you."

She kept the appointment. I worked on her, then turned and talked to her friends while she was in the healing state.

"Do you live in San Diego?" I asked one of the gentlemen with her.

"Oh, no, we flew in from Chicago, and as soon as Nora wakes we'll be catching a flight back."

"You mean you came all the way from Chicago, just to see me?"

"Yes. Friends told us about you."

I was flabbergasted. I had never been to Chicago, and people were flying in from there to work with me.

Just then Nora woke.

"It's gone! The pain's truly gone," she exclaimed. "Gene, I know lots of people in Chicago you could work on. If you say so, I'll organize them and give you a place to stay."

Not having enough money for a plane ticket, I said, "I'd like that a lot, but I'll have to see how things go."

"Let me know," she said, "and I'll set it up for you."

In those days I relied on contributions, and most of them added up to nothing. I told my roommate about the Chicago offer. Although we were flat broke we scraped together enough for a one-way ticket.

When I got to the Windy City, I was well taken care of. Nora kept her promise and found about three hundred people for me to work on. This was a community of Russian immigrants, who gave me a warm, gracious welcome, and we had great healings that weekend.

I remember a little boy who'd fallen off a wall and was paralyzed. The doctors told his mother that the nerves in his spine were destroyed and he would never walk again. I worked on him, and was working on his mother when she let out a little scream. I turned and saw the boy standing up in his bed. Before I left that weekend, he was able to walk. I was touched and delighted that my powers could manifest themselves in such a wondrous way.

The people were appreciative of what I was able to do for them, and showed it with generous donations and a standing invitation to return to them. By the time I left, I was five pounds heavier and had enough money for my return trip and three months' rent on the house in San Diego.

I now had an office, and the self-acknowledgment that healing was my occupation. This was great, but I was still treating it as a hobby, and couldn't get the feel of how to organize it.

I didn't have a set fee; people paid what they wanted. Some gave small donations, while many felt it was perfectly acceptable to make use of my services without giving anything in return. This method of payment kept me in poverty and I was constantly running around trying to get electrical contracting work to subsidize my healing.

I'd often run into people who'd say, "Gene, simply charge a flat fee for your work," and I'd respond with proper indignation: "I can't charge people for partaking of God's gift.

How can you even suggest that? God doesn't charge for anything. This gift belongs to him," etc., etc. If there was ever a wrong time for self-righteousness, this was it.

I was also inundated with the everyday workings of the office: phone calls, bookkeeping, appointments, vendors, bills. I needed help, but I was in no position to pay for it and was at a total loss as to what to do when a charming, middle-aged woman walked in one afternoon.

"Do you have an appointment?" I asked.

"No," she said. "I heard about what you are doing and I'm offering to help."

June was definitely a gift from God. "Will I take you up on that offer?" I asked rhetorically. "Yes. Yes! Now, start now!"

About a week after June started she came in with a newspaper picture of someone dying of AIDS. "Would you work on him?"

"Sure," I said, thinking that she'd never match the guy to the general photo with no name. The paper would probably give her the runaround, and that would be that.

Much to my surprise, she came in the next morning and said, "I got him. Make the call."

"Oh, no, *you* call, this was your idea."

"Okay, I'll call."

She got him on the phone and told him she worked for a healer, whom she thought might be able to help him.

"I don't believe in such things," he said to her, "but what the hell, I'm dying and have nothing to lose. Bring your healer down, and let's see what he can do." John was so weak he was unable to come to my place, and so I agreed to go to the AIDS center in San Diego the next day.

The first time I saw John Lounsburey, two guys were carrying him into a room. He was thin and frightened, and when I asked him to lie down on a table he rebelled.

"Oh, no," he said. "No way. I've lesions on my back that

are so painful I couldn't possibly consider it." He dug in, and was emphatic when he said, "I won't lie on my back."

I didn't say a word, I stood there looking at him. After a couple of seconds he shrugged and said, "Okay, okay, I'll try it."

He got on the table. I started working on him and he quickly went into a meditative state. Some of the medical staff came in to watch, but as soon as the room lit up, they cleared out. The room illuminated a total of three times. About two and a half hours later John opened his eyes, sat up, swung his feet over the table, and looked at me.

"You know, I feel pretty good," he said, and looked around as if he were seeing us and the room for the first time. "Do you think you can get me something to write with?"

"I don't see why not." I motioned to June, and paper and pencil seemed magically to pop out of her purse.

"I want to write about what I experienced while I was asleep," he said, and began to write. When he finished the poem he handed it to me to read, and I would like to share it with you.

White Pillar of Light
Piercing my soul
Engulfing my being
Showering my body with healing energy
Pulsating pain
Driving into my crippled leg
Visions of red liquid
Before my eyes
Rhythmically appearing in
Harmony with the stabbing healing my body
Driving the malady
From my leg.
Fiery flames

Burning my face
Like a severe sunburn
Spirit guides
Removing disease
Energizing the body's own healing powers.
Floating in space
Out of body
Spirit healers
Protecting my being
While body is healed
Warm vibrations
Through my body
Emanating through healer's hands.
Source
Unknown to me
Existence felt
Through sensory nerves.
Subliminal state
Foggy haze
Turning to natural energy
Walking straight, no limp, no pain
Feeling fine
As never before.
Thank you, Creator
For Christ Mind in healer
—John Lounsburey, October 28, 1985

"Sir, if you have the time I'd like to see you again tomorrow at your center," he said.

"Call me Gene," I answered.

John smiled, jumped off the table, and walked out of the room unassisted.

At nine the next morning my doorbell rang and there he was with twenty of his buddies from the AIDS center.

"Hi," he said with a broad smile. "I brought some friends. Could you work on them?"

I looked out the door. I'd never seen so many people in front of my office before. They were mostly young men, some clearly in advanced stages of the disease. I felt my energy level rise and knew immediately that I could help. "Yeah, sure, John," I said. Then I called out, "Gentlemen, come on in and find yourselves a 'piece' of floor."

I was walking, kneeling, and crawling between them when my only paying patient, Jack, showed up for his weekly appointment. He walked in, watched me working, scratched his head, then climbed over the men and went into the healing room.

"What's wrong with those guys?" Jack asked when I went in to work on him.

Oh boy! All the alarms went off in my head. I knew I should have called and told him what was going on. He should have had a choice about whether to come here or not. But, since I hadn't, I decided on the direct approach.

"They have AIDS," I said.

He looked at me with disbelief, jumped up, and made a beeline for the front door. His exit time could have probably made the *Guinness Book of Records*. "There goes my only paying client." I sighed as the door slammed loudly behind him.

Jack hadn't been gone more than five minutes when the phone rang. It was a very tired, dedicated mother calling to ask if I would work on her son, an AIDS victim.

"I'll make it worth your while," Ellen said, "but you'll have to come to my house. He's too weak to move."

I told her about the people from the AIDS center and that I couldn't possibly be there before eight or nine that evening.

"That'll be fine," she said. "We'll be waiting for you."

"Good," I replied as I hung up. Once again, the universe was looking out for me.

Later in the afternoon the phone rang again. It was Jack

on the other end. "I'd like to come back and see you tomorrow," he said.

"I think I ought to warn you, all the guys from the AIDS center will be here again."

"That's okay."

"See you tomorrow," I said and hung up.

The next day when I went into the room to work on Jack, he looked me straight in the eye and said, "Gene, I was really angry with you for exposing me to all these guys. When I left I went for a luncheon appointment with a lady friend. I told her what you'd done and how angry I was. When I looked up she was crying. 'I'm sorry,' I said, 'for getting so emotional over this situation.'

"She shook her head and said, 'That's not what I'm crying about, Jack. I am crying because we'll never see each other again.'

"'Why not?' I asked.

"'Because,' she said, 'I have AIDS.'

"I was shocked at how stupid and judgmental I was. I apologized to my friend and I'd like to apologize to you. I may not be comfortable here with these people but I'd like to continue my work with you."

When I had time to reflect on this I was amazed at how quickly Jack's condemnation of people with this affliction had come back at him. It was a good lesson for him, and one he accepted courageously. My lesson came when I went to see Ellen's son, Joey.

I was close to flat broke, with barely enough money for the gas to get me to her home. Although most people accepted my gift without giving me anything in return, Ellen did pay for my traveling expenses.

It was around 8 P.M. I'd worked all day, but I wasn't tired. I took a quick shower and headed for Ellen's home. When I walked into the living room I saw a young man in the advanced stages of AIDS lying in a hospital bed.

"Who are you?" he asked.

"My name is Gene, and I'm a healer. Your mother asked me to try and help you."

"Are you gay?"

"No."

"Well then, what are you doing here? Get out!" he exclaimed.

I looked at him and said, "Are you a human being?"

"Yes," he said.

"Well, that's what I'm doing here. I am one human trying to help another human."

It took a moment before he smiled, and we eventually became good friends. I went there almost every day, and after a few weeks, he graduated to a wheelchair, then to a walker, and finally crutches. He was doing well enough to think about visiting a niece and nephew in Arizona, and I was very happy for him.

"Joey," I said, "you can do anything you want when you get better, but it'll be a while, because right now you're living on the energy I'm giving you."

A few days later the phone rang and it was his mother.

"You won't believe this," Ellen said. "Yesterday Joey caught a flight to Arizona and had a relapse in midair. They're bringing him to a hospital in San Diego. Would you see him?"

I hung up the phone very upset, thinking, How dare he destroy all the work we did over the past few weeks? He could have had a complete recovery, and now we were going to have to start all over again.

I was angry as I drove to the hospital the next morning. The stern lecture I was going to give him was rolling over and over in my mind. On the ride up on the hospital elevator I was becoming more and more disturbed. I'd decided the first thing I was going to say to him was "You blew it!

How could you do this when we were making such good progress?"

When I got off the elevator and looked out the picture window at the view of San Diego's skyline, I could see a policeman putting a ticket on my car. I watched the guy writing, knowing full well I didn't have the money to cover the ticket, and found the irony of this situation very funny.

So, instead of lecturing Joey, I simply said, "Hey kid, what's going on?"

He took a moment, then said, "Gene, I don't want you to touch me anymore."

My heart filled with compassion. "Joey, I want you to know I forgive you for anything you think you may have done, and I'll support you in anything you might want to do."

He very simply said, "Gene, I want to leave. Please get my mother. I want to tell her that too."

I called Ellen in and Joey repeated his desire. "Mom, I don't want to be here anymore. I want to go."

"If that is what you want, son, I accept your decision."

With that said, Joey closed his eyes and, just as quickly as the switching off of a light, he was gone.

I stood there and realized that this was a lesson for me: that I was never to interfere with free will, that this was God's precious gift to each of us, that we all have the right to exercise it at all times.

The twenty guys were still coming to me. I was spending the day working and charging them nothing. It was getting toward the end of the month, and the rent money was nowhere in sight. I knew that most of these men had no money, but I felt it might be a good idea for them to share in their healing, in very simple ways if necessary. As payment I asked them to bring a piece of firewood or a rolled-up newspaper to heat the house. The next morning, when the doorbell rang, instead of there being twenty guys, there were only nine. I was amazed. I thought to myself, What is more important to them, their health or not sharing in their healing? I was saddened that so many of them were so closed they couldn't participate in the healing process. It truly hurt because they had all been making progress.

I had become so involved in healing that I'd completely lost sight of the practical material things. If I had sat down and thought about who was going to pay the rent on the place, I might not have lost my first healing center. I realized that I had to be responsible to the people I had made commitments to, and I could not do this without asking them to be responsible to me.

Even the church has to pay the oilman and the guy who cuts the grass. Where do they get the money for this? God doesn't give it to them; the people do by taking responsibility for the church.

After losing the center, my thinking about charging changed. I thought, God doesn't want us bankrupt, and I don't think he wants us to be without food or shelter. I believe he wants us to represent him in a fashionable manner and have our needs met without spending our entire existence focusing on the material things.

I decided that it was necessary for people to share in their healing, and I set up a modest fee arrangement. On one of my many healing trips to Europe, I was interviewed on a radio program in Germany and the subject of charging a fee for my services came up.

The interviewer said to me, "How can you charge so many marks when this is a gift from God?"

I said to him, "I am from the United States."

"Yes."

"How do I get here?"

"You fly."

"Do you think Lufthansa says to me, 'Gene, you are a

healer, sit in this seat and we will take you to Germany so you can heal people'?

"No, they say, 'Gene, we want X amount of marks, or you can only heal Californians.' Do you know someone who would be willing to pay my bills? If so, I'll never charge another penny for my work again."

The interviewer, of course, had no answer.

As my mind scanned through the events that had led me to my present situation, I remembered the many lessons I needed to learn in the early stages of my profession. It seemed that each person who came to me presented me with a unique set of problems, each giving me invaluable insight into the human condition. There was a neverending number of problems people had created for themselves. Most of the time they were not aware of their participation in the pain, nor could they easily see a solution.

Sometimes, even when they were shown the way out, they were in such a rut that they couldn't break the pattern and go in a new direction. Many times when the emotional side of the person was understood, the physical problems could be alleviated. Make no mistake, the emotional and physical bodies go hand in hand and are capable of creating some incredible problems when there is a lack of balance.

When I forgot to be watchful and stay in the observer's seat, I would get pulled into the problems people brought me.

I remember one such occasion which involved a lady who came to me for a healing. I just barely touched her and she was out. I couldn't believe how fast she was able to go into a delta state. The only problem was that she just kept going. I realized, as I tuned in on her, that she did not want to stay on the earth, and she had come to me for assistance in leaving. I'd never thought about anyone using healing energy in this way, so I was surprised and concerned.

It took me a long time to get her back. I worked and coaxed and worked, and three hours later I did get her back into her body. The minute she returned I got her up off the table, helped her put on her coat and hat, and firmly escorted her to the door. After that experience, to avoid a repeat of that situation, I decided to put a protective bubble around each person before I started sending energy. Had that lady decided not to return to her body, I would have had her death on my hands, a risk I just wasn't willing to take.

Periodically, after mishaps like this last experience, I would decide to turn off for a while and revert back to electrical contracting. But always, the minute I tried to pull away from my healing work, I'd find myself surrounded by people who needed healing. I'd be walking on the street, a wheelchair would bump into me, and I would find myself silently helping; or someone would bring someone to me and someone else would overhear and ask me to work on another person, and it would snowball. Suddenly there would be a line of people asking me for help. It was always in my face. No matter what I did or where I went, I couldn't get away from it, and so reluctantly I would give in and continue doing the healings.

As I had been skeptical for twenty-five years, I knew nothing about the healing arts, meditation, or nutrition. My second daughter, Annie, had an interest in these areas and she suggested I go with her to some of the various meetings offered by organizations for alternative medicine. As I listened to some of the speakers and took part in some of the meditations, I slowly began to understand some of the things that had happened to me, but I was still having trouble accepting it all. As I look back now, I realize that this lack of acceptance on my part was one of the greatest hurdles I had to surpass. It took a long time for me to accept the fact that I could help people heal themselves and find a more positive way to live their lives.

Sometimes when I went to classes that were attempting to

awaken the healing powers latent in all of us, I would intuitively know that I didn't have to do any of the exercises suggested, as my gift was all there. All I had to do was accept it
and use it.

I was intrigued by the healing process and the good feelings and moments of exhilaration it gave me when I saw
someone who had been sick walk away in good health. I
knew that I had the ability to have a positive impact on many
people's lives, but I didn't understand how or why my presence helped them. When people would question me about
what I was doing, I felt odd and ill at ease. I couldn't carry
on a conversation with them using scientific or medical ter-
minology, so I really felt out of my league. All I knew was
that I could make people feel better, but I didn't know why.

My upbringing had been such that I believed the only
people who worked these kinds of miracles were pious
beings who wore robes and had halos. They led austere lives
filled with strict disciplines and spent a great deal of time
praying and studying the scriptures. Here I was, just an
average all-American, fun-loving guy, who was suddenly
able to perform the same feats as these deeply religious people. I spent a great deal of time in those days trying to find
someone who could tell me why this had happened, but no
one could. Instead, they would put their own limitations
onto me. I met with priests, rabbis, ministers, professors,
and anyone else who would listen, and I'd always ask the
same question: "Why did this happen to me?"

I always got the same response: Everyone I sought out
would shake their heads and say, "I don't know."

The religious leaders would usually tell me to read the
Bible and look to God for the answer. As I wasn't a religious
person, I wasn't sure I had the right to talk to God, and I
kept searching. Some of the organized religions frowned
upon my gift, dubious that it really *was* a gift and implying
that it might be a curse instead. Of course no one could give

me the answer, because it was inside me, waiting for me to discover it.

It was not until I went to a Spiritualist church that I met people who were able to accept the fact I had this gift. They encouraged me to continue to work and let it develop.

Years later, while conducting an Open Eye Meditation, I asked the audience to share what they experienced. A lady stood up and said, "When I looked at you while you were transmitting energy, all I could see was a body of light weaving in and out around your physical form. At times your body was nothing but an expanse of light."

She continued, "At first I thought you came from a spaceship, but you didn't. You were chosen to do this work by a higher power before you were born."

This, I thought to myself, was as good an explanation for what had happened to me as any, and a positive one at that. I only wished I had heard it much sooner: It would have saved me time trying to find an answer that would satisfy me.

At any rate, I was thrust into a situation where I was both doctor and counselor to people from all walks of life. I was having a lot of personal contact with clients who were asking me for advice about their health and how to live their lives. I always had the answer for them, but I didn't know where this information came from.

If someone called me a week later and said, "Now, what was it you told me to do?" the information would no longer be there.

While I was tuned in I would get an insight into what was needed to help a client, but as soon as I passed the information on, it was gone. It wasn't mine and thus was not retained. This is hard for some people to understand. People were coming to me on crutches and in wheelchairs and pretty soon they would be able to walk, and I didn't know why.

Someone would come to me and say, "Hey, I only have a

week to live. The doctors say there is nothing more they can do. You have got to help me."

What do you say to someone in this situation?

I knew any person who had been given a death sentence was frightened, angry, and frustrated. I could sense the helplessness he or she was feeling, and I'd be overcome with compassion and would find myself silently working, trying to help.

When I had time to reflect, I'd be aware of the awesome responsibility involved. The love and compassion I felt for all living creatures and the sincere desire to help people in need seemed to transform the energy that was flowing through me into ever larger dimensions. The more I used it, the stronger it became and the less sleep I needed. I found that I could work eighteen hours a day with little or no sleep, and still feel rested and ready to work. I never turned anyone away, no matter what time of day or night someone called, whether it was a human or animal in need.

At times I would get a call from someone frantic, and I'd agree to see them. Sometimes when he or she arrived at my office and saw me for the first time, there would be a look of surprise, and the person would say something like, "You? A healer? You don't look like a healer. You look more like an auto mechanic."

"Well, they too know how to fix things," I would respond lightly.

Others, especially people who had known me before I had accepted my gift, would look at me and say, "Gene, you are healing people; how are you able to do this?"

I was so baffled and unsure about my abilities that I'd hang my head and say, "I don't know, I really don't."

I remembered the turning point in my acceptance of my gift. It was an incident that happened on Father's Day. That was the day I found the courage to accept the fact that I had been singled out.

I'd been invited to my daughter Annie's home for a Father's Day party in her backyard. When my son John pulled the car into the driveway, I got out and headed toward the back door. I was about to knock when I heard Annie scream. It was a shriek of terror. Alarmed, I grabbed the door and, without thinking, broke it down. When I entered the kitchen I saw Annie standing in the middle of the room with her two-and-a-half-year-old son, Anthony, in her arms. He was bleeding profusely, his scalp badly torn.

"What happened?" I asked.

"He tried to pet one of the dogs," Annie said, "and they attacked." My daughter was reeling; I knew she was about to faint. I grabbed Anthony and ran.

When we got to the emergency room, the doctors on call took one look at Anthony's wound and shook their heads.

"We can't do anything to help him," one of the interns said. "The damage is too severe; only a plastic surgeon can take care of this."

"Well, then get us a plastic surgeon!" I said.

"You need an appointment to see a plastic surgeon, sir; they're not on call."

"Well, then call one," I shouted. "Surely you can see that this child is in need of immediate medical attention."

"We'll put a call in and see if we can locate one," the other intern said. "Meanwhile, you can wait in one of the cubicles on the side of the emergency room."

I followed the intern to the cubicle. Knowing there was nothing that could be done to speed up this waiting process, I sat patiently awaiting the arrival of a plastic surgeon. As we sat there waiting, I saw that Anthony was about to fall asleep. I glanced up at Annie. She was staring at me and smiling.

This was cause for concern. I was sure she was going into shock, but as I followed her eyes and looked down at my grandson, I saw the bleeding had stopped. He was completely quiet, which is extraordinary for a two-and-a-half-year-old. Aside from whimpering "Mom" a few times, he stayed quiet and didn't struggle to get out of my arms. When the plastic surgeon came, he looked closely at the boy.

"What a mess. This is going to take a while. Why don't you put him on the table here, so we can get started," he said.

"No way," I answered. "I'll hold him and you do what you have to."

I knew the doctor couldn't give him anything to deaden the pain and that if I held on to the boy his suffering would be less, much less.

Anthony received too many stitches to count and only cried out a few times. Today my grandson is unscarred and he's not afraid of dogs.

This was the experience that made me fully accept my healing gift. I had been able to help my grandson and lessen his pain and suffering by giving him the energy that flows through me.

There was no more flip-flopping back and forth from the electrical contractor to the healer. I was now a healer, period. By this time I had met a lot of people and I was continually being invited to various places to do healings.

I met Michelle from Los Angeles who wanted me to come there, do healings, and conduct meditation classes. Although I didn't enjoy the commute, I went willingly. As time passed I found myself going there on a regular basis and, after traveling back and forth for about three years, I decided to open another center, this one in Santa Monica, a Los Angeles suburb.

I put out to the universe my need for a place to do my work, and a short time later I found a small house in Santa Monica. It was about a twenty-minute trip from LAX airport and ideally fit my needs. The house had three bedrooms, which I turned into healing rooms; the living room became the waiting room and the kitchen became my office.

I was now asking a modest donation of twenty-five dollars, so I could pay the rent and take care of my material needs without any difficulties. As I became better known, people started inviting me to visit other cities in the United States, and then Europe.

I realized that there was much healing that needed to be done on this planet, and I accepted the invitations and began traveling to the people. Sometimes it was a hardship for me to cover the travel expenses, but I continued.

It was during this time that I kept hearing a name spoken to me in my mind. The name was Egidio. I had never heard this name before and it sounded strange to me. At times it would be spoken over and over: Egidio, Egidio, Egidio. Sometimes when it was spoken to me in numerous succession, I would see an ethereal face forming. It was a man with a receding hairline and tiny ears tucked close to his head. He had a kind expression on his face and he was always smiling at me. As I looked at the image, I would always feel a friendly warmth flowing through me. I was starting to become obsessed with this name and its mystery, for I didn't know what it meant. I would ask people I ran into if they knew anyone by the name Egidio, or if it meant anything to them, and the answer would always be no.

One Sunday afternoon I decided to pay my sisters a visit. After I'd been there for a while, I started hearing the name Egidio in my head, and this time it didn't let up. The sound became so loud I felt it might be audible to my sisters.

"Do either of you hear anything?" I asked casually.

"No," they said in unison. "Why do you ask?"

"Because I keep hearing this name, Egidio, and it's so loud, I thought maybe you could hear it, too."

They looked at each other and then burst out laughing.

"What's so funny?" I asked.

Anna Marie picked up the family photo album and

thumbed through it until she found an old piece of paper that was frayed around the edges. She handed it to me.

"What's this?" I said as I took the paper from her.

"Read it."

As I examined the paper I saw that it was my birth certificate, and on it was the name Egidio. It was the formal name given to me at birth.

"Interesting," I said as I stared at the paper, "but this can't be the whole story. I keep seeing a vision of this man. He has a receding hairline and very tiny ears. Do you have any idea who it could be?"

"It doesn't ring a bell," said Antonette.

Anna Marie continued to thumb through the photo album. Finally, she found a picture of my parents standing with a man and handed it to me.

"Who is this man standing with our parents?" I asked.

"That is the healer who helped Mom get rid of the tumor she had before she carried you. She was so impressed with his healing abilities that she asked him to be your godfather."

"And his name was Egidio Pasqualie," said Antonette.

The man in this picture was the same man I had been seeing in the visions I was having. As I looked at the picture, a calm peace settled over me.

"So Egidio Pasqualie was a healer and my godfather, and our parents decided to name me after him."

"That's right," said Anna Marie. "Now you can understand why we found your story so amusing."

"Yes, yes, but I am more interested in the facts. Egidio Pasqualie was a healer and now I am healing. You know, I think I'm going to take the name Egidio for my healing name."

"Why do you think he passed his healing gift on to you?" Anna Marie asked.

"I don't know. Stranger things have happened," I answered.

"It is a nice way to acknowledge and honor your godfather," said Antonette, "and, after all, it was the name given to you at birth."

"I'm glad I came over here. This not knowing who Egidio was or what it meant was becoming a perplexing preoccupation that was beginning to consume more and more of my time. I want to thank you for clearing this situation up for me."

"I'm glad we knew your history, so we could help," said Anna Marie.

From that day on I have used the name Egidio. I liked the sound of it, it felt right to me, and it became the symbol of my new life. I left the electrical contractor behind forever.

Finally I came back to my present reality; I was in Leningrad and in less than five hours I was going to be doing healings on crowds of people. I knew I had to get some rest and got into the big white fluffy bed and closed my eyes. Time passed and I dozed off.

The First Step Toward Destiny

I was awakened in what seemed like a very short time by the sound of people in the other room. I opened my eyes and saw that dawn was breaking in this strange country where I didn't know the language or the customs, yet I was comfortable with the realization that I had to be here.

I got up, bathed, dressed, and went into the dining room. There was a quiet air of happiness and peace that reassured me about the good feelings I had about being here.

"Katrina and Dmitri have gotten together a group of people for you to work on," Maria told me, as I sat sipping my cup of tea at the breakfast table.

"We have asked some of our friends to come and experience your healing energy," Katrina told my interpreter, "and we found the perfect place to do it, in the Hall of Heroes."

I figured I'd be taken to some historic building with a lecture room that would hold fifty to a hundred people, but to my surprise, when we reached the Hall of Heroes, the structure was a majestic theater.

We climbed beautiful marble steps that led to a magnificent entrance, went through two gigantic swinging doors and there we were: on a large revolving stage, framed with heavy rich velvet curtains. The room was luxurious, with three-tiered balconies draped in velvet, and when I walked down the aisle I could feel plush carpet under my feet. It was a splendid room, built to accommodate a large number of people, but it wasn't equipped to do the work I do.

"Gene," my interpreter said, "Dmitri and Katrina want to know what you are going to do and how you want to do it, so they can instruct the people."

I looked out at the sea of faces and I too wondered. I'd always worked on people while they were relaxed and reclining, because they were more receptive to healing in that state. How *was* I going to work on all these people in the time allotted to me without the facilities usually offered?

I knew I had to make a decision and fast, so I matter-of-factly said, "Let's put the people in every other row. That way I can walk behind them and give them energy by touching them on the back of the neck."

It was a long day and I went through a thousand to fifteen hundred people.

On the second day, I said to my organizers, "There's got to be an easier way. There are too many people in too short a time. It took much too long."

Someone suggested, "We can put chairs on the stage and have the people file up in a single line and sit in the chair."

"No," I said, as I pondered the situation. "Tell you what, let's have fifty volunteers come up and form a horseshoe on the stage facing the audience. Then have the people in the audience come up in groups of fifty and stand in front of the volunteers. Tell the volunteers that they will be 'people catchers' for the day."

"People catchers?"

I decided I had better give these people an explanation for my horseshoe arrangement. "Yes, that way if some of them go into a deep meditative state and begin to waver or lose their balance, they'll be caught by the person standing behind them."

My interpreter looked at me with raised eyebrows and

then relayed my message to Dmitri and Katrina. They too had peculiar looks on their faces.

I continued, "Sometimes when people are very sensitive, a heaviness comes over them, and they have the need to sleep. I don't want anyone to fall if they have these sensations."

My interpreter translated what I had said to Dmitri and Katrina. They nodded and set about organizing the people without a word.

Normally I work on ten to sixteen people, with two to five people in a room. I ask them to lie on a cot, then cover them with colorful Mexican blankets that utilize all the energies in the color spectrum. I give them one and a half to two hours in a meditative, or the more powerful delta, state. But with the vast numbers of people I had to work expediently, trying to give them a maximum amount of energy in a minimum amount of time. I knew this could be accomplished by working exclusively on two of the major power points—called chakras—the heart chakra to open up their hearts and the forehead area to bring up their consciousness. Those two areas include every major chakra in the body. I knew by focusing on those two areas they would receive a complete healing.

I instructed my organizers to put chairs on one end of the stage for the people who could not stand, and I had them select volunteers who'd act as escorts for the people who wavered while standing.

The morning went well. As I went around the horseshoe and past the chairs, I saw this beautiful picture-perfect child with bows in her hair, a full face, and big curious eyes that stared up at me. I went to touch her on the shoulder and she lunged at my hand and grabbed my pinkie. She slid off her mother's lap and stood on the floor looking up at me with big trusting eyes. I said to myself, I am going to take this child for a walk around the circle. She held tightly to my left pinkie as I did the healing with my right hand. When I came full circle back to where her mother was seated, I looked at her mother and she was crying. Maria was also crying.

"Why are you crying?" I asked.

Maria said, "Her mother told me she is five years old and because of a prior illness hasn't been able to walk until today."

A little girl who hadn't been able to walk for five years was now trotting across the stage, walking with me. Walking without a hint or indication that she was infirm in any way.

She was holding tightly on to my pinkie and smiling. I said to myself, Gene, whose hands are these anyway? I knew it was not for me to understand, but rather to accept.

The child slipped her hand into my shirt pocket, found my last Tootsie Roll, and ran across the stage to her mother's lap. I'd brought these candies for the children I was going to visit, but, being the biggest child of all, I ate most of them. Anyway, it was a beautiful moment, and remains an incident that stands out clearly and happily in my memory.

There were many instances where people almost instantaneously rid themselves of ailments. I realized the Russian people were very sensitive. This was probably due to the fact that they were not allowed an open spiritual life and were forced to turn inward. The result was the development of a rich and deep inner sensitivity to all things spiritual. These people joyously received my energy without any skepticism. It was a long, rewarding day; I'd worked on approximately seventeen hundred people.

Maria approached me with a woman smiling through her tears.

"What's wrong?" I asked.

"This woman wants me to tell you how happy she is to see the Russian people participating in a healing ceremony openly. She never thought she would see this in Russia, and she is very happy."

I patted the woman on the arm and mused to myself, Little do these people know I don't have permission to be doing these healings.

I wasn't uneasy about this situation, as intuition was telling me it wouldn't be a cause of trouble for me or any of the participants. It was an exhilarating feeling to see these spirits literally being unshackled, not only on the physical but, more important, on the emotional and spiritual levels; those are the levels where the shackles are truly shaken off.

Although we worked hard, there was time for some fun too. My interpreter arranged for several sightseeing tours of historic Leningrad. I was also introduced to a TV anchorwoman who wanted an interview with me for a national TV show.

"If you can meet me in the basement of an abandoned church, I would like to tape an interview with you," she said.

I thought about it for a while and decided I had nothing to lose. "Okay," I said, "I'll be there."

I went to the location I had been given, a totally deserted and isolated place. It was a little spooky, but I decided to wait, at least for a while. After what seemed an eternity, I saw a lone figure making its way toward me. The body got closer and I made out the silhouette of the anchorwoman.

"I am sorry," she whispered, "I could not get away. I was called to do a story on a UFO landing."

"Oh?"

"Yes, and I would like to know what your opinion is on UFOs. Do you think they are real, or are they just something people imagine?" The tape recorder began to roll.

"Oh, a lot of people I talk to think they're real," I answered.

"We have reports of UFOs landing here periodically, and I was just wondering, is this happening in other countries too, or is it just in Russia?" She was very serious. She didn't really know whether we were experiencing the same thing in our country or not. At the time there was an iron curtain around any information that might affect the government.

"There are people all over the world who claim they have been abducted," I answered.

She was breathless and still whispering into the mike when she said, "There was a UFO sighting and landing less than a week ago in a town north of here. Children who were playing in a schoolyard were abducted out of the schoolyard in broad daylight. There were adults in charge who stood by helplessly, watching in disbelief."

"Are you joking?" I asked.

"No, this really happened. Are there people in America having the same kinds of experiences?"

"There are people who say they have been abducted and write books about the experience, but to my knowledge, there's never been anything as blatant as a ship landing in broad daylight and taking children. Are there other incidents like the one you just described?"

"Yes," she said, "several similar to this one have happened in places scattered throughout Russia."

"Can I get more information about this?"

"Not really. Anything that does get recorded is blacked out for whatever reasons the government has for not wanting the people to know that such things are happening."

"Records should be kept; you never know when this might come in handy."

"Do you keep records of these incidents in your country?"

"Well, yes and no. There was a project that began as Project Sign and later became Project Blue Book. It was produced by the United States Air Force and it attempted to give a reasonable explanation for approximately thirteen thousand sightings that were reported by Americans from 1947 to 1969," I said.

"So your government acknowledges the existence of UFOs?" she asked.

"Well, not really. They basically tried to explain away the sightings as weather balloons, swamp gas, secret weapons from other countries, and the like. There are private groups who do try to document sightings. They feel that the air force is not telling the people everything they know."

"What do you think?"

"I think UFOs are probably here, for whatever reasons."

"Do they want control of us? Is that why our governments vehemently deny their existence, because the aliens have already contacted members of our governments and our governments think the people would go into mass hysteria if they knew?" she asked.

"Maybe. When people set out to deceive one another, the reasons can sometimes appear rather complex, but it is usually for some type of personal gain at the other person's expense."

"So you think members of the government have made deals with them, like, we will let you experiment on our citizens in exchange for your advanced technology?"

"That could be a possible scenario. If they are doing experiments on people, I think the key words might be *genetics* and *cloning*. It's ironic when you stop to think about it. We want the technology that was developed by their superior intellect and they want our DNA, which is charged with an unpredictable emotional body," I explained.

"I mean it would be one thing if they only took people who volunteered for these experiments, but when they take a random selection of people against their will, it is another thing. Is there anything we can do about these abductions?"

"Apparently not, but I will tell you I feel one of our human weaknesses might become our greatest strength in surviving their uninvited visits. We humans have the ability to change from an emotional state of peaceful happiness to raging anger in the flash of an eye, and the aliens don't understand or know how to deal with that kind of energy."

"Have you had firsthand experience?" she asked me cautiously.

"No," I answered, "what I tell you comes from an inner spontaneous knowing for which I can offer no concrete proof."

With that we dismissed the subject of UFOs and went on to discuss the various facets of illness.

"When you get sick, how do you go about curing yourself?" I asked her.

She hesitated, then said, "It depends on the illness."

"When you look at me, what do you see?"

"I see Gene Egidio."

"But how do you see it?"

"I just see it, through my eyes."

"In other words, you see a picture, don't you?"

"Yes, I see a picture of you."

"What would happen if you saw a picture of yourself in excellent health, jogging or running or playing volleyball or swimming? If you saw that picture, what would happen? You saw yourself in maximum health and the color on your face was good and you radiated the well-being and happiness that is everyone's birthright."

"I guess I would feel really good about being in excellent health," she replied.

"That is what you need to do every day. Just take a few minutes every morning and evening to picture yourself being in maximum health—because what is an illness, but a picture you have in your mind of what you were told you have. If you change that picture around and make it the way you want to see it, there will be a vast improvement in your health."

We next talked about everyday problems, because no matter what language we speak, or where we are, we have the same everyday problems that we have to deal with in some fashion. This, of course, gives us a common bond.

When she realized that I had the same problems she had, we were able to share the ways we dealt with them. By the time the interview was over we had concluded that the only difference between us was the fact that we uttered different sounds to express ourselves.

"I want to put this interview on national TV," she said, "but I will not be able to use everything we have discussed."

I smiled and said, "It's universal, kid—that's why we have editors."

She returned my smile. "I'm glad you understand my situation."

Then she suddenly became serious. She took hold of my arm and said in a whisper, "Can you help me stop smoking?"

"Sure," I said.

"But how? What can I do to stop?" she asked.

"Just don't put a cigarette in your mouth," I said.

She looked at me and started laughing. She laughed so hard she dropped her portable mike.

I waited until she stopped, then said, "Let me tell you a story. I used to be a very heavy smoker. Not only did I smoke three packs of cigarettes a day, but I also smoked five cigars and I always carried a pipe in case I ran out of tobacco. One night I was sitting in my living room reading the paper and smoking a cigar when I became aware of my oldest daughter, who was seven, sitting in the corner of the living room sniffling and then she began crying. I put the paper down and went to her.

"'Diane,' I said, 'Whatever is wrong?'

"'Daddy, you're going to die.'

"'No I'm not. I am going to be here for a long time. What makes you think I am going to die?'

"'I know you are going to die because today in school they showed us a film, and the people in the film said that when you smoke your lungs turn black and you fall over and die, and Daddy, you smoke a lot. I don't want you to die, Daddy, because I love you.'

"I took the cigar I was smoking out of my mouth and crushed it in the ashtray. Her plea for me to stop smoking profoundly touched me and I never had the desire to smoke again.

"I credit this wise seven-year-old child for saving my life, for she broke me of a very bad habit in an instant.

"The story does not stop here, though. You've heard the saying, What goes around comes around? Well, that is what happened in this situation. When Diane was eighteen she came home one night with a cigarette in her mouth.

"I looked at her and I said, 'Diane, do you have a cigarette for me?'

"'Daddy, you don't smoke,' she answered.

"'Do you remember why I don't smoke? Do you remember what you said to me when you were seven, about my lungs turning black and then I would die?'

"Embarrassed, she put the cigarette out, and she has never smoked another one to this day.

"If you want to stop smoking, just stop for one day. You can do that, can't you?"

The anchorwoman nodded her head.

"Okay, you stop smoking for one day, and the next day the person who stopped smoking for one day must also stop smoking for one day. Then the person who stopped on the second day must then stop smoking for one day. The person who stopped smoking on the third day must stop smoking for one day, and keep this chain going, and you will find that you will never need to smoke a cigarette again, and you accomplished this by only stopping for one day."

"That's an interesting way to look at this problem," the anchorwoman said. "Okay, I will give it a try."

"Good," I said. "I don't think you'll be disappointed."

One interesting note on this interview was the fact that after the discussion of UFOs, I learned that two UFOs had landed in the vicinity close to Leningrad that very evening.

It just goes to show what the thought process can manifest: By acknowledging the possibility of the existence of extraterrestrials, we were suddenly able to bring them into physical existence, ship and all. Our mental observations and thought forms had quickly manifested into a physical reality for all to see.

The Orphanage

When I was deciding my itinerary with Dmitri and Katrina, they asked me if I would like to go to a children's orphanage.

"Sure," I said without hesitation.

They paused, and a short conversation ensued between them and my interpreter.

"They just want you to know before you get there that this is an orphanage for 475 mentally disturbed children," my interpreter said, looking to see what my reaction was going to be.

"I am getting good feelings about going there," I responded.

"Good, then we will make the arrangements."

The day arrived for us to go to the orphanage. It was in a country setting, and we had the privilege of a very pleasant drive along the outskirts of the city. We took a scenic route, going around the bay, always keeping one of the many waterways in sight. It was a breathtaking view. The architecture in Leningrad is surely some of the grandest in the world, and this city truly did deserve the nickname the Babylon of the Snows.

The majesty of the structures that made up the skyline had obviously been drawn up by men who had envisioned the joyous ecstasy and rapturous bliss of the spiritual and had the technical skills to turn that vision into a physical manifestation for all to see.

Peter the Great was the one responsible for putting the plans in motion for the creation of these splendid structures. He'd traveled extensively in England, France, Germany, and Holland in the 1700s, and he had been greatly impressed by the majesty of Western culture, especially the architecture. When he returned to Russia, he resolved to bring the grandeur of the West to his own doorstep. This was one of the first cities in the world to be planned before being built. Not just the buildings, but the canals, waterways, and layouts of the streets were planned. He then imported the people necessary to go along with the buildings—the aristocrats, artisans, and merchants. No expense was spared, as can be witnessed by the dome of St. Isaac's Cathedral. One hundred kilos of pure gold was used to gild this dome, and when the sunlight hits it, its sparkling magnificence is capable of transporting one to another dimension. As I drank in this luxurious sight, I became aware that there were no wooden structures.

"Why don't I see any evidence of wood used in any of the buildings?" I asked my interpreter.

"This city was built under the supervision of Peter the Great, and in order to ensure its longevity, he forbade anything but stone to be used. If anyone used so much as one beam of wood in any of the buildings and was caught, he was automatically banished to Siberia," Maria explained.

"Well, these structures have definitely withstood the test of time."

"Yes, his vision was far reaching. Unfortunately, a lot of people lost their lives in order for his vision to come into being."

"I'm struck by the number of religious structures."

"Yes, the Russian people were a deeply religious people, and still are."

As we drove on, I spotted a small church in an isolated area. "Are services still held in that church?" I asked.

"No, it is more of a museum these days. We can stop and go in if you like."

"Yes, I would like that."

My interpreter told the driver to stop. I got out and went up to the door of the church. When I took hold of the handle the door slowly swung open. As I stepped into the church I could feel the energy from yesteryears, and it was good energy. I was glad I had stopped. There were small gray candles about the size of lead pencils there, so we each lit one and put a donation in the donation box, and then continued on our way.

When we reached the orphanage I saw that it was a lone building standing in the middle of a pasture. What an appropriate place for an orphanage, I thought, a dwelling surrounded by nature on all sides. The pastoral mood would surely have a calming effect on the children, and at the same time give them a place to play that was void of the industrial pollution found in the cities. We pulled up to the front of the building and a well-dressed gentleman came out to the car. The expression on his face was stern, yet it held a gentle kindness.

He introduced himself as the director of the orphanage and gave us a hearty welcome.

I got out of the car and extended my hand. "I'm Gene Egidio," I said, smiling at him.

He beamed a big smile back and said as he shook my hand, "I'm Yuri Borisov."

Everyone was introduced and Yuri invited us into the orphanage. As we entered the main hallway of the building, I noticed several people scurrying around and they all had big smiles on their faces. This gave me a good feeling about what was going on there. Yuri invited us into his office. It was obvious from the decor that he was a true believer of the Communist way: There was a bust of Lenin and various pictures of other Communist leaders. He indicated for us to be seated. As I sat down he smiled and, through my interpreter, started spouting Communist propaganda. Yuri thought the Communist philosophy was a work of genius, especially the commune, where everybody was supposed to share every-thing with everyone.

"It's good to share what you have with your neighbors," he told me.

I nodded. Not unlike the Christian teachings left us by Jesus, I thought silently to myself.

I listened awhile to what my interpreter was translating and then I got up, went over, and patted Yuri on the shoulder.

"Yuri," I said, "all this talk is not necessary among friends. I am here for the children. What can I do for them?"

"Ah, we have been preparing them for your arrival," he said. "If you will just follow me, I will take you on a tour of the orphanage now."

"Fine."

As we walked through the various wards, Yuri would talk to my interpreter and she would tell me how many children there were in the ward, what their goals were, and what their needs were.

I was rather impressed with their program. These were all children who were either mentally or physically impaired, and the goal of the orphanage was to teach these children how to function in the outside world. Their training program was ingenious. They had set up mock stores, streetcars, and buses to teach the children how to buy the goods they would need to survive and how to use the transportation systems that would be available to them when they became a part of society.

They also had job-training programs. The girls were being taught crafts, knitting, and the operation of the machinery necessary to make clothing. For the boys, there was training in the use of tools in carpentry, general con-struction, and autos. In one room they had computers. There they were teaching computer skills to the children with less severe impairments. I was told there was a shortage of computers, so the training in that area was limited.

As I went through the wards, Yuri would tell the children to go to their dorms, lie on their beds, and wait for me to come and give them energy. The children thoroughly enjoyed what was going on, and the exchange of energy between us was great. When Yuri saw what a good time the kids were having, he allowed me to have as much time as was needed to work with the children.

When we got to one classroom the girls were making beautiful macramé.

They showed me their work, and I commented, "These are really beautiful. You should take them to the marketplace and sell them. You could use the funds to buy more computers."

When my interpreter told Yuri, he laughed and said, "Ah, Capitalists."

Maria told me what he had said and he and I both laughed.

We, of course, were approaching this idea from opposite viewpoints. In his mind he was thinking that all Capitalists think about is a way to make a profit, and in my mind I was thinking what a shame it was that these children were being held back because of the embracing of a set of ideals which excluded the use of Capitalistic practices, even when they could be beneficial.

He knew my beliefs were totally opposite his, but still he treated me in a friendly manner and let me know he was willing to work with me.

We continued on our rounds of the orphanage. As I went from ward to ward, I saw that the children were well treated. It was obvious that many of these kids would achieve a major accomplishment if they only learned to take care of themselves; at best, they would be able to make only a limited contribution to society. Nevertheless, these children were treated with respect and they were a very happy and well-mannered group.

We went into one of the larger rooms that had been converted into a playroom, and when Yuri got the children's attention he said, "Children, today I have a surprise for you. A man from America has come here to visit you, so what do we say to our guest?"

The children responded in unison and in English: "Hello and welcome."

I responded with a big smile. "Well, hello there," I said. "Are you playing a game?"

They smiled and giggled and squealed with delight.

I knelt and picked up a block next to one little girl and handed it to her. As she took it, I patted her on the back. She responded happily by hugging me. In this moment we both got a healing, as there was an exchange of good positive energy. We healed mentally, when our auras expanded and touched, and then physically, through the magnetic charge we received from making physical contact.

As I went around the room and worked on each child by a hands-on approach, I could tell Yuri was pleased that the children were enjoying themselves. I talked to each child with the help of my interpreter, and my presence in the room made it possible for every child to continue receiving healing energy after the initial physical contact. Working with children is a little different from adults. Usually my healing energy makes adults feel sleepy, but it's often just the opposite with children. They suddenly become charged with a lot of energy and the result is a display of excessive physical activity on their part. All in all, it was a pleasant day and we all had a good time.

When I finished working with the children, I said, "Well, how about you, Yuri?"

A broad smile came across his face, and through the interpreter, he said, "Oh, I am far too busy today."

My hand was resting on his shoulder and by the time he finished his sentence I'd given him a healing.

He looked at me and said, "You know, I suddenly feel very sleepy. I think I am going to have to lie down."

I smiled and nodded my head understandingly. His need to lie down was the result of the energy I'd transferred to him. He was in a healing state for about an hour or so, and when he woke he came running down the hall to catch up with us.

He motioned for me to sit down and hurriedly explained to Maria, "Tell him to wait here, I will be back in a few minutes."

I nodded and said, "I'll be here when you get back."

When he returned he had his family with him. He looked at me and smiled with trust in his eyes. "I would like for you to do to my family what you did to me."

"Okay, next in line," I said with a smile.

I gladly received his acceptance of me and my work. Here was a man who, in embracing Communism, had given up the worship of God but was still capable of transcending his beliefs and accepting me.

I motioned for his family to sit down. "Now it is your turn," I said, as I started working on his wife. I worked on his entire family for about three-quarters of an hour. The orphanage director stood by watching, smiling from ear to ear.

When I finished working on his family, he invited us to dinner, and it was excellent. He was able to afford meat, and there were homemade noodles and a really delicious soup.

As we made our way back to Leningrad I felt good about the day, and we had been invited back, so that meant the feeling was mutual.

As the news of my work at the orphanage spread, people

began to come to see me. The next day a woman brought her son, a young man of about twenty-four, who had a very bad speech impediment. I worked on him for about an hour and a half. When he came out of the healing state, he was able to speak without a trace of the speech impediment.

His mother was ecstatic. She turned to me and asked, "How are you getting back to Moscow?"

"By train," I answered.

"I will get you airline tickets. It will be faster than the train and more comfortable."

"That would be nice," I said.

Because of the expense and the incredible amount of red tape one had to go through to get tickets, I hadn't bought them, and I didn't think she would be able to get them either, so I dismissed it as a generous offer but nothing more.

Two days later she contacted me. "I have the tickets," she said. "When would you like to pick them up?"

It turned out that she worked for the Mariinsky Theater, where both opera and ballet are performed. As she was responsible for booking the travel arrangements for the ballet when it went on tour, she knew several people who could help her get the tickets, and very good tickets at that. We sat in the front, in the pilot's private reserve seats. The trip back to Moscow was smooth and without incident, all thanks to this generous woman.

We landed at the Moscow airport in the late evening and headed to our hotel. I was looking forward to a hot bath and a good night's sleep.

When we got to the hotel, the KGB was stationed as the entrance. I would have to say that this hotel was pretty well guarded. You had to be identified by the KGB before you went in.

At the desk the clerk held out his hand for my passport. I gave it to him, thinking he was going to check it and hand it back, but he dropped it into a box without even opening it.

"Wait a minute. I need my passport back," I said.

"Sorry," he said, "hotel rules: You don't get your room key unless you give us your passport."

I looked at Maria, who shrugged. "Rules are rules," she said.

The fleeting thought of losing my identification and never being able to get out of Russia crossed my mind, but I was so tired that I decided to take a chance.

"So, do I get my key now?" I said, smiling at the clerk.

"Sure. The bellboy will take you and your luggage up. Just follow him."

"Thank you," I said. As I turned to follow the bellboy, I pictured a hot bath just minutes away.

When we got to the floor where our rooms were, we said good night to each other and went our respective ways. I was in my room about five minutes when there was a knock at the door. I opened it and there stood a small lady with a child in one arm and a rolled-up newspaper in the other. She quickly started speaking a barrage of Russian to me and pointing to her child with the rolled-up newspaper.

"Whoa, whoa," I said, "let me get my interpreter," and I motioned with my hand for her to wait.

She stood patiently by my door as I strode down the hall. When Maria and I got back to my room I invited her in.

She was plainly dressed, in a long brown skirt and dark sweater over a simple white blouse. Her long hair was pulled back and clipped with a tortoiseshell barrette. She wore no makeup, but had a healthy glow about her. She carried herself with an air of determination but, at the same time, she had a look of worried concern on her young face.

"I heard about what you did in Leningrad," she said. "You made the birds fly, and you worked on many people and helped them."

I smiled and nodded.

"My child is sick and I would like for you to see if you can help her. The doctors don't know what is wrong with her," she continued.

I smiled and obligingly took the child in my arms. She was probably about three, but she was not daunted by being given to a stranger. She allowed me to hold her and smiled warmly at me. I worked on her for about fifteen minutes, then I put her down on the couch, as I sensed she was going to fall asleep. When she awoke about forty-five minutes later, I picked her up. I could see her chakras were in perfect alignment and gave her back to her mother. She smiled and thanked me in Russian. Then she handed me the rolled-up newspaper she had been holding all this time.

"Thank you," I said, as I took the package from her.

After she left, my curiosity got the better of me and I decided to see what was inside the newspaper. When I finished unrolling one layer of paper there was another layer. After I finished unrolling three layers of newspaper, there in the center was a smoked fish—head, tail, and all. I looked at it, then turned to Maria.

"That," she said, "is a Russian delicacy. You will eat well tonight. The area of Russia that lady comes from is four hundred miles from here and it is known for its smoked fish."

"You mean she carried a child in one arm and a fish in the other for four hundred miles?"

"Apparently so," my interpreter said, as she smiled at me.

"Well, I am very impressed, but I have to confess that I find it unnerving to think of eating something that is staring at me. Maybe you would like to take it."

Her eyes lit up, then she said, "Oh no, this is a gift to you for the work you did on her child."

"We can share."

"Okay, I will take it and fix you a plate without the eyes staring at you."

"Good enough," I answered.

These kinds of nights were prevalent. In fact, I was told

that the people rarely slept more than two or three hours during this time of the year, as the white nights were at their height, which meant almost twenty-four hours of continuous daylight.

Moscow

On the first morning of my stay in Moscow I met Pyotr Stroganov. He had agreed to find places where I could work during my stay in Moscow. My client in California met Pyotr on one of his many business trips to Russia and put us in touch with each other before I left the States.

As I greeted him, he said, "I have gotten some people together in the basement of my apartment house, and I would like you to go there and work on them before we go to the athletic club."

"Okay by me," I said.

"We have told the chauffeur and he is waiting to drive us there now," Pyotr said.

"Well, let's not keep him waiting," I said as I headed toward the car.

When we got there, I was led down into the basement of the apartment house and through a winding narrow hall. When we reached the end of the hall, Pyotr knocked on a locked door. Soon someone opened it and let me in. The door was quickly closed and locked again.

I thought to myself, How peculiar. Why all this hush-hush and secrecy?

There were more people there than I could work on in the half hour allotted to me, so I spoke a few words to them and then I put a chair on the table, climbed up on the table, and sat in the chair.

"I am going to do an Open Eye Meditation," I said.

I knew these people didn't know anything about meditation, so I could just imagine what was going through their minds.

"You probably think I look odd sitting on this table, don't you?" As I looked out at them I saw slight nods of agreement here and there. "Well, there is a reason for my actions. I am sitting on this table so I can see each one of you. The purpose of the Open Eye Meditation is for me to send each of you energy, but instead of doing it by hands on, I am going to send you the energy through my eyes.

"Now, be sure and look directly at me, for if you are not looking at me, you won't get the full benefit of what I am going to do." They had puzzled looks on their faces, but I hoped they would understand after they got into the experience.

I sent each person in the room energy three times. When I finished they were like kids in a candy store. They were all whispering and laughing and pointing and giving up little *oohs* and *ahs*. I always ask the audience to share in what they experience during the Open Eye Meditation for it is always different with each individual, and they gladly complied with my request.

"I saw Jesus standing directly behind you," one lady said, "and his body consisted of pure white light, but even though his body was white light, I could still make out his features, and it was definitely Jesus."

Another lady stood and said, "I saw an angel standing directly behind each person in the room."

A third lady said, "Well, I didn't see any people, but by the time you finished, the whole room had filled up with white light, and it engulfed all of us."

I was very pleased with the results. They were so enthused about this experience that I invited them to come to the athletic club where I was going to spend the day doing healings. They were very happy about the invitation and those who could said they would be there, so we disbanded the meeting and proceeded to the athletic club.

When we reached the building I turned to Maria and exclaimed in amazement, "This is a church, not an athletic club."

"It used to be a church," she replied.

"Why would they turn a church into an athletic club?" I asked, as I gazed at the beautiful building with its huge stained-glass windows.

"So the people won't have a place to worship," she answered.

"How sad."

"When we entered, we found about four hundred people waiting to see me. My supporters grabbed my arm and pulled me out of the room.

"What's the matter?" I asked.

"We must all go, now!"

"But why?" I asked.

"If you value your life you will leave now. The KGB could raid this place at any time, since you don't have permission to conduct a meeting involving so many people."

"Well, I have nothing to hide," I said, "and since I am already here I am going to go for it."

Maria looked at me with alarm and concern.

"Anyone who is uneasy about being here can leave," I said. "I am going to stay, but each of you must do what you feel is best."

With a shrug of resignation, my interpreter sat down. That meant she was staying. I waited for a couple of minutes and then I said, "Don't worry, we all are receiving help and protection from the universe." She smiled.

I turned to the people and said, "I am not here to teach you and I am not here to sell you anything. I am here to support you in whatever you believe."

When my interpreter finished giving them my message, there was loud applause; these people totally accepted what I was doing. We went through four hundred people by early afternoon, and then we picked up two hundred more, because by that time, the people had gone home and told their friends to come.

During my first session there I worked on a woman who, after she came out of the healing state, told me she was a medical doctor, and she invited me to the hospital where she worked.

"I'm sure my colleagues would be very interested in experiencing what you do."

"Fine, I would like very much to visit your hospital," I told her.

"It's on the outskirts of Moscow. Just tell your chauffeur; he will know how to get there."

"Will do," I answered.

The next day I found time to go to the hospital. She wanted me to demonstrate my healing abilities, so I did the Open Eye Meditation for her and several members of the medical staff. They were all sitting around a table, so I didn't have to worry about anyone falling. When I finished the meditation, I went around the table and did a quick hands-on healing for everyone in the room. When I got to the doctor who had invited me, I was guided to put my hands on her eyelids.

As I did this, she let out a little gasp.

I jumped back, startled. This gasp, I knew, was the result of the unexpected twinge of energy she had received when I put my hands on her eyelids. When she'd come to me the day before she had a small tumor on one of her eyelids. As I looked at her now, I saw the tumor was gone.

"Do you have a mirror in your purse?" I asked her.
"Yes."
"Please take it out and look at your eye."

When she did so, she let out another little gasp. "The tumor is completely gone!" she exclaimed.

"Yes, it is," I said.

"My God!" she said. "You must go through our hospital wards. There are many people there who could benefit from your healing abilities."

That was the beginning of my working in the hospitals in both Leningrad and Moscow.

After leaving the hospital, I went back to the athletic club to continue the group healings I had scheduled.

After my last session that day, a man came to me. "I was at your morning session and was so impressed with your work that I went to the managers of the club and received permission for you to use the gymnasium tomorrow. It will be quieter and there is more room," he told me.

"Why, thank you. I appreciate your help," I said, as I looked at my interpreter. She gave me a nod, indicating that she felt this move would be okay.

So the next morning when we returned to the athletic club, we went directly to the gymnasium.

When we got there, there were approximately fifteen hundred people lined up and waiting. The line extended outside the building and was spilling into the street. I was later told that some of the people had been waiting for hours, and I was struck with the patience of the small children in the line. They stood quietly beside their parents, not causing the least bit of trouble. I was surprised and delighted. I knew it was going to be a challenge to work on fifteen hundred people in such a short span of time, but I went to work and saw all of them by day's end.

In the midafternoon my interpreter approached me with a robust white-haired gentleman and said, "This man wants to know if you would like to be interviewed by him. He says it will only take a few minutes. We could take a break. He'd like to do this interview under the trees in front of the building."

"Sure, I would like to talk to you," I said, extending my hand to him.

He shook my hand and smiled. He had a cameraman and a soundman with him, and we followed him to a shaded area under the trees.

First he explained that he had his own TV show, which appeared once a week on the State channel. Then he turned abruptly, looked me straight in the eye, and asked, "What are you doing here in Russia? What business do you have being here?"

"I am here to support and help your people with my healing abilities," I answered.

"Explain what you do in the United States."

"I have two healing centers, where I work on people and teach classes on meditation. I live in California, and my two centers are in Santa Monica and Encinitas."

When I said "California" his eyes lit up. I could see he identified with it, even though he had never been there.

"How do you know someone is ill if you don't know exactly what is wrong with that person?" he asked skeptically.

I pointed at the soundman and said, "He has a problem in his chest," and I pointed to the place on his chest where I could feel a problem.

The interviewer turned to his soundman and asked him if he had a problem in his chest. The man nodded. "How did you figure that out?" the interviewer said, turning to me.

"It is a knowing I have. I don't know where it comes from or how it works, but I do know it is always there and almost always correct. Sometimes the time line is a little off, but that, of course, corrects itself with the passing of time."

"It is very interesting," he said. "Thank you for the interview."

I smiled and said, "Well, I guess we have now built a bridge between our two countries."

He said sadly, "A bridge is great if we can go two ways on it," meaning that I could come to Russia, but he could not come to the United States.

The soundman put his hands over our hands and the interpreter put her hands over his, so we had a building of hands to cement our relationship. It was a very nice way to end the interview, I thought. I went back and continued doing the healings. My interviewer watched and participated.

When I finished healing one woman, she took an envelope from her pocket. "Please mail this for me when you have a chance," she said.

"Is it a letter to a relative?" I asked.

"No, it is a letter to the Red Cross asking for medicine for my child and any help they can give me," she replied.

"Okay," I said, "I will mail this letter as soon as I get to the United States."

I approached one man in military uniform. As I glanced at him, I pondered whether he was here to be healed or to check me out. When I looked at him and put my hand on his neck, he returned my gaze and smiled. I will never forget that smile. There was an instant connection made between us.

I should explain here that when people are sitting in chairs, one of the best points on the body to send the healing energy to them is at the base of the neck where the spine begins. Here the energy can travel down the spine and work on all the chakras, as well as on the head area.

During the course of the healings I was compelled to look back at this man. It was about an hour and a half later and he was just coming out of the healing state. He looked at me and gave me a thumbs up. So, jokingly, I gave him two thumbs up. He grinned and that was the last I saw of him that day.

It was early evening when we finished with all the people.

Everyone wanted to go back to the hotel and rest, but I'd seen a poster advertising a circus.

"Is that poster current?" I asked my interpreter.

"Yes," she said, "the circus will be playing here for the next week."

"I want to go." They looked at me with disbelief.

"After working on fifteen hundred people, you want to go out?" they echoed. "Aren't you tired?"

"No," I said, "as a matter of fact, I feel rejuvenated. I thought we did good work today and I feel very satisfied about how things went."

"But you gave energy to so many people; how can you have enough left to do anything else?"

"I don't give away my own energy," I said. "The energy I send to people is from the universe and it is merely passing through me, as I pass it on. I really want to go to the circus. I think it would be a pleasant way to end the day."

My companions nodded wearily and off we went. It was a magnificent performance.

The next morning, before I left my hotel room to go back to the gymnasium, I felt compelled to bring one of my Power of Love T-shirts. I folded it up as small as I could, because I had a limited number, and if I gave one out, there would be fifty more people who would want one. I knew I just had enough for everybody who was helping me.

The chauffeur, whom my organizers had arranged for me to have throughout my stay in Moscow, always had his daughter with him. She was a beautiful child, about ten years old I would guess, who was severely paralyzed. She could only move her lips and her eyes and was unable to speak. She could, however, communicate on other levels. Her eyes were very expressive and she had a beautiful smile. Every morning when I got into the car, I would talk to her and work on her at the same time.

"This morning let's play a game of hide and seek. I have

something in my hand and you indicate which hand you think it is in," I told her.

She smiled and turned her eyes toward the hand she had chosen. She was a delightful child, and she was always eager to cooperate with my requests. I knew every time she was in my presence she was receiving energy, and I wanted to help her as much as I could in the short time I spent with her.

There was a rapport developing between us and I began to look forward to the ride each morning, just to see this beautiful child light up with happiness. Her sweet angelic smile made a deep impression on me, and I wanted to pass on some of my gift to her. She knew it too, because she always smiled at me with an expression of gratitude and warmth, and would watch me as I left the car, until I was out of sight.

This morning when the chauffeur arrived at the gym, I looked out the window and saw throngs of people. The police were there directing traffic, and military troops were helping.

When the chauffeur stopped the car, who should open the door of my car, but the military officer I had worked on the day before.

He looked at me. I smiled at him and pressed the T-shirt into the palm of his hand.

"This is for you."

His eyes filled with tears, but he was determined not to give in to the emotion. Instead, he put his arm around me and, without saying a word, walked me through the crowd, up the stairs, and into the hall.

There were probably two thousand to twenty-five hundred people there.

As I looked around the hall, I noticed there was a dotting of military personnel with their families, and I found out later the man I had worked on the day before was one of the commanders of the Twenty-seventh Division of Moscow. I then realized why the police and military were directing traffic instead of taking people away: He had cleared the red tape and made it possible for me to do my work without any interference from the government.

What a beautiful day I had! People left, radiating happiness.

We had national coverage every night on television for the week, although I am not sure what was said. It turned out to be positive, because it really opened up the people to the wonderful healings we were performing.

One military officer brought his wife and child with him. Due to a birth defect, the child had a lip that was two to three times its normal size. They came every day. In three days it was down to its normal size. The officer and his wife were overcome with joy. They were crying and laughing and embracing one another, and then the officer shook my hand and hugged me.

"I'm glad I was able to give you this moment of joy," I said, returning his embrace.

Another officer brought his daughter to me. When I looked at the man and his wife, it was obvious they were pouring a lot of love into the child, but she still had health problems.

On the third day I said, "Everything is where it should be. Your little one is going to be healthy."

When he heard this, he started to weep, then took a medal off his shirt and pinned it onto mine.

"No, no, no," I said, "that is yours. You should keep it."

But he wouldn't take it back. I learned that the Russian people are very giving and they get insulted if you don't accept their gifts.

After taking a cue from my interpreter, I finally accepted the medal.

"Thank you, I will keep this always."

He beamed at me and then scooped up his daughter and left.

"You have just received an Olympic Silver Medal," my interpreter said. "I'm sure that medal meant a lot to him, and his giving it to you shows great admiration for you on his part."

I smiled, touched by this generous, self-sacrificing act.

People gave me rare coins, their grandmothers' pins, and one lady gave me her earrings when I stopped the pain she was experiencing in her body.

I was beginning to wonder how I was going to get out of the country. I had been given so many articles that my carry-on was beginning to look like a pawn shop.

My Sleepless Night in Moscow Continues

As I stared out of my hotel window, I realized my stay here was about to come to an end. I glanced at my watch and saw it was now 3 A.M. The night was still very bright, but I had to get some sleep. Tomorrow it would be time for me to leave the U.S.S.R. and go back to my home in California. I was both happy and sad about this.

I closed my eyes and tried to imagine a dark night sky, hoping it would help me drop off.

I awoke abruptly at 6:35. I knew there was much work to do and I felt the need to get my day started. It was now time to pack all the gifts the people had given me. I had many pieces of jewelry and rare coins and I didn't know if I'd be allowed to take these things out of the country.

We anticipated a lengthy time going through customs and arrived at the airport early. Just as I was about to walk up to the counter the man came over to me.

He pointed at me and said in broken English, "You go to a different area."

I looked at him and felt my heart sink. He was a tall, over-sized, burly guy with a scrubby beard and what we would refer to in America as a GI haircut. His large appearance and the scowl on his face made him look very intimidating. This, plus the gruffness of his voice, sent chills through me.

Oh, boy, I thought, this is it. I'm going to get the third degree.

I had just watched the customs officials literally rip apart the suitcase of the man who was in front of me. They had found nothing, but when they finished with the suitcase there was no lining left in it.

I had not bothered to wrap any of the gifts I had been given, so I thought to myself, Just wait until they see the inside of my carry-on luggage. Who knows what they'll do to me. Some of the gifts would have made the eyes of any pawn shop owner sparkle with excitement.

As I started to walk in the direction the customs official had instructed me, he came out from behind the counter. "Give me your bag," he commanded.

I said nothing as he took the bag and put it on his shoulder. He then put his arm around me and walked me away from everybody.

Am I in hot water or what? I said to myself.

Finally, when we got out of earshot of the crowd, he extended his hand.

"I know all about you and I want to shake your hand," he said with just the flicker of a smile on his face.

It was a very firm handshake. Nothing halfhearted about this guy, I thought to myself. Whatever he believes and commits himself to is done 100 percent.

"I want to thank you for what you did for my people," he said. "And as a token of my appreciation I want to carry your bag for you to the plane."

Was I ever relieved when I heard that! I smiled and said, "That is a very nice gesture. You know, I really did not want to come to the Soviet Union, but I am very glad I did. The people here have been wonderful and I know I'll be back."

He nodded.

As I turned, he waved to my traveling companions and his friends. As they started toward us, he opened a gate and we all went through. That was his gift to us: making it possible for us to avoid the long customs line. He and my friends surrounded us and escorted us to the plane. Because he was an officer, no one bothered to question his authority.

This was my first visit to Russia, and it was a very rewarding experience.

It taught me a great deal about who people really are. They are not Russians, Americans, Germans, or Communists; we are all one family. These labels are just tags we give each other. People, regardless of the country they live in, are just that—they are people, and they are the same throughout the universe. The Soviet Union is a country filled with many wonderful, caring people, and they have great respect for those among them who have highly developed intuitive abilities.

I have since returned to Russia eight times, and each time was a unique and totally different experience. I must say I did have a little chuckle when I visited the orphanage in 1994. The government had cut their budget and, in order to bridge the gap, they had given in to the Capitalistic ways. They were selling the macramé.

Section Two

My Healing Life

To heal is to love. The universe and everything in it, including humans, exist because of love. When a person acknowledges this and strives to create a life filled with love, he or she is happy, and this in turn causes the quality of life experienced to be full and rich in meaning. Put simply, any situation looked at through the eyes of love, no matter how grave it is, will be solved or accepted more easily than when this energy is blocked out. Actually, there is only one principle we need to follow to live life to its fullest, and that is to live consciously in a state of love and use the foundation block of happiness as the cornerstone on which to build our life experiences.

I understand now that to help another human in the healing process one must have unconditional love and compassion for all living creatures. It is necessary to understand and accept the set of circumstances that brought the person to whatever predicament he or she is currently experiencing.

There is an alarming absence of compassion by many who practice the healing arts today, especially those who choose the path of conventional medicine. This scientific method is touted as the superior way but is cold and rational and only concerned with treating the physical body while the spiritual body is totally ignored. This is one reason there has been an increase in alternative healing methods. Many have become aware of the one-sided treatment procedures in our medical institutions, and they have begun the search for a way to keep the humanness in their lives. People say to me, "When I go to a medical doctor with an ailment, I am tested instead of treated." Sometimes these tests are numerous and lengthy and the suffering ignored until all test results are in. More and more people acknowledge the fact that treatment in a warm, loving, and supportive environment that acknowledges and gives nourishment to both the physical and the spiritual body is an aid to the restoration of good health.

When people ask me for an opinion about whether or not to use conventional medical methods, I always tell them to take the best of both worlds, for both conventional medicine and alternative healing methods have value.

As I continue to get more and more experience healing people, I realize that human behavior is, in actuality, very simple. People act out of either love or fear. When people act out of love they are open to, and receive a constant flow of, universal energy that is everyone's birthright. They are in a state of expansion and are happy. When people act out of fear, they become cut off from the universal flow of energy or, at best, the flow becomes blocked at various points in the body, and they then experience the onset of illness. Fear may take many paths. It is this emotion that keeps us from listening to our inner self, so we end up creating all kinds of problems for ourselves. When a person acts out of fear, you can be pretty sure there is a state of imbalance present in the person's life. This causes every cell in the body to cry out for the correction of this imbalance. If it is not corrected we have the onset of physical symptoms, which will eventually manifest disease. There is considerable truth in the statement that disease is merely "dis-ease."

Because of the gift of free will, we have the ability to change what we think and feel and thus bring about a balance between the body and spirit. The vehicle for achieving this balance is the mind, for it has the ability to be the intermediary between the body and the spirit. We have been given the ability to reason, think, and create. This ability to create is a very important tool, for it has the capacity to visualize something that does not exist, and this new vision can be brought into existence if we exercise free will and choose to manifest this new thought form.

When we make time for quiet meditation, we open the door to the infinite knowledge that is ever present in the cosmos and will be given to us in flashes of insight. These sudden moments of revelation can be called "gut feelings" or intuition. If we can learn to trust our intuition and bring the knowledge we receive in this manner into our everyday lives and make the decision to use it wisely, we can create the inner balance that is necessary for perfect health. When we have reached a state of inner joyfulness that we can carry with us throughout the day, even in times of adversity, we can be relatively sure we are heading in the right direction for the pursuance of perfect health.

Unfortunately, many people don't do that, for they are not sufficiently in tune with their spiritual self to know what they need, and the mind is truly the great trickster. It can conceal the fears in many complex ways or cajole us into believing that nothing is wrong; then we manifest habits that contribute to ill physical or emotional health. The habit of excess is an example: eating excessively, dieting excessively, drinking coffee excessively, smoking cigarettes excessively, or any other activity done in excess.

Another habit that wreaks considerable havoc is denial. An example of this is the unhappy person who emphatically denies that he is able to change the undesirable situations in his life so that he can experience happiness. When confronted, he insists he is powerless and has no control over the situations around him. God gave all of us access to the universal flow of energy. It is within us and unless a person has made the decision, whether consciously or unconsciously, to let an outside source control him, he is indeed in control of his own life.

Many times people seek conventional medical treatment for an ailment and the problem is alleviated, only to return months or years later. Why? Because the thought pattern that created the illness in the first place wasn't addressed. It's not enough to treat only the symptoms of an illness. The root cause must be found and eliminated, or the illness will either return or manifest itself in another form. This is where meditation becomes very helpful. If a person can reach deep inside her spiritual makeup to understand what caused the illness in the first place, and then have the courage to release the thought pattern, she is truly on the path to a more joyous way of living that is disease free.

Often people who are having physical problems cannot remain quiet long enough to realize the healing ability that lies within them. That is where my skills are needed. My role in the person's healing process might be described as jump-starting. When I work on people the current of energy that is present in my essence is transferred to them. This helps them ignite their own life force, and at that moment they bring forth their own healing energy from within their own bodies to continue the healing. Some people are more focused and adept at working with their healing energy than others, and that is why some have more complete healings than others. The mind plays an important role in this, and if people are willing to make the effort to change the thought processes and behavior patterns that led to their problems, they will usually have a successful healing.

Many people who have successful healings continue to come to me periodically. It is like taking your car in for a tune-up. These people usually have a good outlook on life and understand the healing process, and know the value of these "tune-up" healings.

It is very important for people to realize that all healing

comes from within. Of all the universal laws relating to healing, the most basic law, and yet the most difficult to understand, is the law that no person heals another person. Yet, in contrast to this truth, by making an attunement within ourselves, we can bring that attunement to others and that can help facilitate their healing. We can't give what we don't have, but we must be willing to give what we do have. For it is in helping others that we are healed. I would go so far as to say that there can be no healing unless there is a response of the body consciousness to whatever outside influence the person is allowing himself to be exposed to. Unless there is a response to the external influence by the life force within the body, there can be no healing.

As we meditate and awaken our higher consciousness, the level of attunement we achieve can be passed on to others. There must be a flow out of the self for the healing to be accomplished. As I said before, we cannot give what we do not have. We understand that principle at the material level, but we don't apply it very well at the spiritual level. We go to the gym and work out and spend millions of dollars on proper diet, all for the purpose of maintaining our physical body, but what do we do for the spirit? It is just as important as the physical body, and it must be attended to in order to bring about the balance we need for perfect health.

If we are to heal others we must first heal ourselves, and it is up to us to take the responsibility for this. The healing of self is accomplished by the raising of the spiritual vision and vibration, and it is imperative that we make a sincere and wholehearted attempt to achieve this, not only for ourselves but for everyone on the planet.

Many times people will come to me with the attitude, "I dare you to heal me, just you try and I'll show you!" These people receive the same initial "jump-start" that everyone else gets, but what they do with it remains to be seen. They usually don't want to take the responsibility for their own health so they fail to continue the work.

It is more important to them to be able to say to me, "See, it didn't work. You can't heal me." That of course is their choice. They have exercised free will.

I cannot stress enough the importance of taking the responsibility for our spiritual well-being. We are complete and whole entities, and the universe is asking us to stop being children and become evolved adults. Once we have raised our own level of spiritual awareness, we can pass it on to others and so facilitate their healing. Like an unbroken chain, that quickened spiritual vibration needs to reverberate around the world, to help all those who wish to receive the healing. As we raise that attunement in others, we give the planet an opportunity to reach a new stage in its evolution.

The healing energy I send a person distinguishes what the person needs, almost like a built-in computer. Regardless of whether a person comes to me with an emotional, physical, or spiritual problem, I give them the same energy, and it does what is needed. The healing itself is a totally personal matter for the particular person who is experiencing it. Whatever level they need to experience, they will experience, for there are no boundaries. Everybody who comes to me for a healing is healed, some more than others, some less than others. People ask me if one has to have faith. The answer is no, but at the same time there is nothing wrong with faith. It isn't the degree of faith you have that gives you a good healing, it is what happens at the moment I send the energy, whatever it is, that determines what will happen. Some people are healed in one sitting, others take longer.

Any sickness, whether it is cancer or a stubbed toe, is just what we think it is, and whatever we tag it, we act accordingly. I always say, "Don't name it, so you won't have to claim it."

A lot of people think back and say, "I don't know why I got this illness, especially cancer. I have never smoked or drunk, and with all things considered I have lived a very clean, happy, and healthy life. And here I sit with cancer. I don't know how to deal with it. I know what the medical profession tells me, but when I ask for guidance from my higher self I don't receive an answer and I become very confused and frightened."

I met such a lady in a bookstore in San Diego early in my healing career. At this time I didn't have a center, so I had ended up doing healings in the back stockroom of this bookstore. The owner of the store came to me and told me a customer had come in who had shown her a cancerous tumor protruding from the side of her throat, about an inch or so outward. I talked to the lady for a while, and she told me how frightened she was and how much she loved life. She said she wanted to be here for her children. I was very impressed with her love of life, and as I placed my hand over the lump without touching it, I continued to talk to her about her mental anguish. I told her the first thing she must do was to stop giving the problem strength by dwelling on it.

I worked on her for about forty-five minutes very intensely, and then I left the room for maybe two or three minutes. When I came back, I had to do a double take, as I no longer saw the tumor protruding. I thought it could have settled down in her throat; I wasn't sure. I worked on her for another fifteen minutes and then I sat at the side of the room, being in the moment. About two hours passed and she finally came out of the healing state. We talked for a while and then she left the room.

Suddenly, I heard the owner of the bookstore give a little shout. I ran to the front of the store to see what the problem was, and there stood the lady I had worked on with no tumor on her throat. We were very happy for this lady.

Three years passed, and by this time I had a healing center in Santa Monica. One day I got a phone call from this lady.

She said, "I would like to come and see you on Saturday, because I have a lump on my left breast now."

"You of all people know what we can do with it," I replied.

"Yes," she said, "that's why I am coming up Saturday."

"Great. I'm looking forward to seeing you," and with that I hung up.

Saturday came and passed and she didn't show up. The next working day she called again.

She said, "Gene, I went to the hospital and had my left breast removed."

I was speechless. I couldn't say a thing. I can't to this day remember what else she said. I do remember her saying that she was coming up the next Saturday because she had found a lump on her right breast, also.

"Okay, fine," I answered.

I said to myself, Now here is a person who experienced her own miracle and she does not trust in herself to go that route again. What really happened in her mind?

I had to remind myself of free will, and the fact that we all have different paths to take. Yet it was a tough pill for me to swallow.

The following Saturday came and went and still no visit.

Two weeks later I got a call from her and she said, "Gene, I want to come up in about a week or so, because I want you to tune in to the aura around my body. I had my other breast removed, and I'm hoping everything is okay now." Once again I was speechless.

She eventually did show up for a healing. I wanted to ask her why she went the route of surgery after she had seen the miracle that she created for herself three years ago, but I couldn't ask the question. As I said before, we all have our own choices to make, and until we change the image in our mind of the explanation we are given about certain diseases, we live with the belief system that is instilled in us. It is really like not believing in yourself. This was my lesson as well as hers: to accept what we believe about ourselves.

In other words, when you come out of the department store, whatever is under your arm, you own. So whatever you accept is what you will become.

Information about the Healing Process

When I do mass healings and work on many people for only a short time, I work exclusively with the heart chakra, to open up the emotional body, and the head chakra, to expand the consciousness. By focusing on these two chakras, all the major chakras receive some attention, as they all are connected to each other.

Before I go any further, I would like to take this opportunity to explain just what a chakra is. *Chakra* is a Sanskrit word meaning "power point." There are millions of power points in our body, but we usually concentrate on the seven major ones, which are located along the spine. These power points are circular indentations and have been described as whirlpools of swirling energy. It is through these power points that the vital energy from the universe flows.

When I do an extensive healing on people and there is time, I make sure their chakras are perfectly aligned. This creates a state of harmony between the physical and spiritual bodies. The body needs three kinds of energy to work perfectly: food for digestion, air to breathe, and a constant flow of vital energy from the universal force. So when we have these elements, we have the possibility of having perfect health.

We spend enough time on the issues of nutrition, and we

know that exercise increases the supply of oxygen to the bloodstream. And through efforts to raise people's level of consciousness during the last two decades, we have become increasingly aware of the damaging effects polluted air has on us and our environment, an issue that still needs much work, if we are to keep this planet the green jewel of a planet it originally was. However, we don't realize the importance of receiving this vital flow of energy that comes from the universe, and a great number of people totally ignore and/or deny the spiritual side altogether, as their sixth sense is not developed enough to see this finer energy.

When we are born we start living in our root chakra. This is our survival chakra, and it is the "cave man" aspect of life, or life at an instinctual level. The basic energy necessary for survival is received by this chakra from the earth and the sun.

As we grow and continue to develop, we start to live out of our abdominal chakra as well as our root chakra. The abdominal chakra forms us on a physical level, and we develop physical reflexes, such as walking.

As we continue to develop we reach the solar plexus chakra, which creates intelligence. This is intelligence that is formed within our body, not within our brain. This chakra, as well as the next two, is receiving energy from the astral forces that man attracts to himself through his emotional makeup.

As the next step in our development process, our heart chakra comes into play and we begin to distinguish between emotions such as love and pain. In other words, our emotional body is now functioning.

The throat chakra basically deals with things we see, hear, and say, but mostly it deals with what we say, so speech is learned. As we continue to develop, we learn how best to utilize this method of communication, as in the art of diplomacy and discernment, for, make no mistake, those who learn to choose their words wisely will go much further than those who neglect to develop this skill.

As we come to the brow chakra, or the "third-eye" chakra, we invoke the creation of intelligence and the opening of the consciousness. This chakra only comes into play after a considerable amount of conscious work toward developing spiritually.

Finally, we reach the crown chakra, which is the most important, for it is the spiritual chakra. This is the chakra that makes it possible for us to receive and transmit information to our higher self and it is the chakra that determines how our individuality is formed.

When these chakras are in perfect alignment we experience a state of balance and harmony between the body and spirit. The more spiritually developed a person is the larger the chakras become. This allows a greater supply of vital energy to flow into the body. It is also worth noting that whenever a person's crown chakra becomes highly developed, it reverses itself. In other words, it is no longer a depression which receives, but instead, it becomes a beacon radiating out, giving the divine light to all who enter his or her presence.

There are many healing stories I would like to share with you, as each story is in itself a lesson in the understanding of human nature. There is not enough space in this book to include all the stories, so I've chosen a few to illustrate some of the many facets of human nature I have encountered in my healing journeys. As I stated before, not everybody gets healed. There are various reasons for this, among them the need for people to have that experience in their destiny path. By the same token, people who do get healed are getting the lesson of experiencing which they were meant to have. You will see in the upcoming chapters how the thought forms created by your mind end up in the body, because the body is the receptacle of the mind.

The Lady with the Green Hair

One of the most far-fetched stories that reiterates how much our belief system controls us is a story about a woman who was literally starving herself to death. She just couldn't eat anything, and there was no rhyme or reason for her problem, either medically or emotionally. I was asked to work on her, and because she was so physically weak, I had to go to her home. She invited me into her living room, motioning me to sit on her long white couch. I chatted with her awhile and, as I looked at her, I kept seeing a bright green light around her head extending down to her shoulders. I couldn't figure out why I was seeing that green. I kept asking her questions and then I had a second sense.

"What happened on this couch we're sitting on?" I asked.

She looked at me for a long moment and said, "Nothing."

Again I asked, "What happened on this couch?"

She paused and then looked me straight in the eye. "My husband killed himself on this couch," she replied.

"When did you dye your hair?" I asked.

"I don't remember," she said.

"Well, try to remember, because I think it has something to do with the problem you're having now."

She hesitated and finally said, "I dyed my hair two weeks before my husband killed himself."

It was interesting to me to see how she related that time sequence—her dyeing her hair and his death.

I said, "The problem is your hair."

She looked at me incredulously, as if to say, You're crazy.

"What do you mean, the problem is my hair?" she finally managed to stammer.

"Because every morning when you get up, you look into the mirror and you see the blond hair and it brings back the memory of him killing himself. It shuts you right down," I said. For a long moment she stared off into space and seemed temporarily to forget I was there.

"Why don't you go out today and get your hair dyed back to its natural color and see what happens to your health?" I said.

A week later she called me. "Well, you were right," she said. "I can now eat anything I want, and best of all I'm hungry and I enjoy eating again."

She thanked me and I wished her well, and as far as I know she has never had any more problems with eating. With that healing I didn't place a hand on her. As you can see, healing takes place on all levels.

Depression

One of the most common and recurring problems I run into is a problem manifested by the emotional body, and it goes by the name depression. Many people come to me and say they are very deeply depressed.

Just what is depression anyway? I'll tell you what it is — it's a thought.

Depression is usually created when we somehow or other end up giving our power away. When we get into situations where we allow other people to control us, and we feel we are helpless to do anything about the outcome and when it's not the outcome we want, we usually find ourselves becoming depressed. Without thought we cannot have action or, put another way, thought is the primary thing that we must do in our life to create action. When people tell me they're depressed I play a little game with them.

"Hey, look up at the ceiling," I say casually.

"Okay," the person responds.

"What's that?"

"What are you talking about, what's what?" says the person as he or she scans the ceiling.

"Is that a ceiling?" I ask.

"Of course it's a ceiling."

"Well, how do you know it's a ceiling?" I ask again.

"Because I was told it was a ceiling. I learned it a long

time ago. The space above me is defined in any dictionary as a ceiling."

"But how do you really know it is a ceiling?" I ask again.

"I can *see* that it is a ceiling."

"But how do you know it is a ceiling?" By this time the person is getting pretty aggravated, so I know I have his or her attention. Usually the person will say something like, "Okay, I give up, how do I really know it is a ceiling?"

And I say, "Because you *think* it is a ceiling. If you didn't think it was a ceiling, it probably wouldn't stay up there."

"Okay, so what does that have to do with being depressed?"

"Well, what did we just find out?"

"I don't know, what did we find out?" the person responds, exasperated.

"I'll tell you what we found out. We found out that you have to think to create a thought about anything. So what does that tell you?"

"What?"

"It tells you that if you are depressed, you are creating it. So now that you know that, it is up to you to create some different thoughts. If you do it every day for a certain length of time your new thoughts will replace the thoughts you had about being depressed. You can also create happiness. It too is a thought."

I then share with the person a story about what happens when we let this thought process get out of hand.

Should I or Shouldn't I?

In our fast-paced society, many people are living in a way that causes them to lose sight of the real purpose of their lives. The result is that they experience life from a state of off-centeredness, and along with that comes feelings of anxiety and depression. At this point, many people contemplate suicide. A well-groomed woman with this problem came to see me at my center one day. I greeted her and asked how I could help.

She said, "I flew in from Las Vegas today, just to see you."

"That's nice," I answered.

"I bought a gun before I came here," she said.

"Why would you do that?" I asked. "This is a safe environment."

She looked at me and said, "Well, I am not happy, and I am thinking about committing suicide."

I looked at her for a long moment, then said, "I only have one question."

"What's that?"

"Do you pay in cash or by check?"

"What difference does that make?" she queried.

"If you kill yourself after you leave here and you pay me by check, the check won't clear and I'll get stiffed," I answered.

Her brow furrowed and her face filled with rage. She

exclaimed in a loud voice, "How can you think of money at a time like this?"

The money, of course, was not what I was thinking about. I was silent as I continued to look at her and suddenly she began sobbing uncontrollably.

Because of a trauma in her life, she had lost the sense of center she needed to maintain to be a happy, well-balanced person. By my asking her a question that put her in touch with her anger, I gave her the vent she needed to release it. After she'd stopped crying, I talked to her and helped her release all the rest of her pent-up anger. In the healing I perfectly aligned her chakras, so she could again experience the feeling of being centered. She was able to leave my center smiling.

Normally when people leave I ask them to leave their crutches or wheelchairs or whatever behind, but I didn't think having a gun hanging on the wall would look so good, so I didn't ask her to leave it with me.

My Cruise on the Nile

In the spring of 1992 I took a trip to Egypt. This was meant to be a healing journey, but we decided to make it a sightseeing trip also, so we organized a group of sightseers and off we went.

The second part of the trip was the legendary cruise down the Nile on a passenger ship traveling approximately seven miles an hour. After about two days on the ship, everyone had lost track of time. The slowness of the pace had changed our tempo, and we were thoroughly enjoying this quiet peaceful feeling that we were experiencing.

While having breakfast, I noticed a couple pushing a young man in a wheelchair, who were very attentive to the young man's every need. When they saw me, they came to my table and introduced themselves.

"We are from Japan," the man said. "When we heard about this trip you had organized, we decided to take it, just to meet you."

The man, who was American, then introduced his Japanese wife who, although her English was broken, spoke well enough that we could have a conversation. "This is my son in the wheelchair," she told me. "He was in a terrible accident, and he fell from a three-story tower."

"I'm sorry to hear that," I answered.

"You are our last hope," she said. "When my son fell he

smashed every bone in his lower torso from his hips to his toes."

"Bones can be set," I said.

"The doctors couldn't set his bones because they were so badly mangled," she answered, "so they decided to fuse them, and in doing so they made it impossible for him to move his knees and ankles. What is worse," she continued, "is that he is now addicted to prescription drugs.

"Please work on my son," she said. "Maybe you can help him. The doctors cannot undo what they did to him."

After breakfast I went to their cabin. He was in bed, and for good reason. Everyone in the group was sick from the contaminated water they were using on the ship. As I approached the bed he opened his eyes and sat up, and his mother introduced me to him. His name was Kichimo. He could not speak English, but his stepfather translated what he said, and we were able to have a short conversation.

He smiled and said, "I want to walk again."

I smiled back. "I'll try to help you."

I could tell from his facial expression that he was very determined, and I knew there was a good possibility that I'd be able to help him. I worked on him for about fifteen minutes. He went to sleep, but I could tell he was aware of what was going on around him. I stayed for another fifteen minutes, until he fell into a deeper sleep.

"Let him rest as long as he needs," I told his mother, "even if he sleeps through his meals."

The next morning while I was at breakfast, Kichimo entered the dining room on crutches, walked to my table, smiled, and bowed. I was pleased to see that he had discarded the wheelchair.

His mother came to my table and said, "He slept through all his meals yesterday, and when he awoke, the first thing he asked for was his bottle of painkillers. I brought the medicine to him. He opened the bottle and threw all the pills into the wastebasket." She continued, "He got through the night without any painkillers, and he wants to thank you."

"After breakfast I will work on him some more," I said.

A short time after I'd worked on him we pulled into port. The group was planning to leave the ship for some sightseeing, and he announced he wanted to go too. On his crutches, he managed to get off the ship and into the bus. When we got to the site, the tour guide found a young girl who was using a donkey to carry water to some men working on one of the temples. He asked her to carry Kichimo to the site we were going to, and she gladly did. I could tell he was in tremendous pain, but he had the courage to go with it. He did not go back to his painkillers, and as I continued to work on him each day, I could see he was becoming more determined to walk.

On the last day of the cruise I told his parents I thought he would be able to walk again, but it would take more time. I invited them to come to my center in California after the tour was over, and they accepted my invitation.

Two months later, they arrived in California. I found them sleeping quarters close to my center, and we continued the work we had begun in Egypt. This went on for four weekends.

One afternoon I said to Kichimo, "Tomorrow I am going to videotape you walking from your bed to the door."

He smiled when his stepfather told him what I had said.

The next day I brought my camera. By this time he was able to raise and bend his legs and turn his ankles. I know this defies all conventional rules, as his bones had been fused, but that just goes to show you what the strength of courage and determination can do.

His problem was manmade, and the question was whether or not he could undo what man had done to him. I pulled his wheelchair up to the bed and said, "Get in the wheelchair, go over to the door, and then get up and walk back to your bed."

He smiled and did as I bid him do. When he got to the door, he raised himself up out of his wheelchair, walked slowly back to his bed, and sat down on it.

Everyone was speechless, but smiling. Kichimo had succeeded in accomplishing what he set out to do, with a little help from me and a lot of guts, pain, and faith in himself.

Bob Takes a Journey Through His Body

One afternoon as I was finishing up my last healing session of the day, I walked over to one of my clients. She was just coming out of the meditative state. I sat down next to her and waited for her to become fully awake so we could talk.

"Your energy field looks very good," I told her as I checked the alignment of her chakras.

"Yes, I feel fine physically," she said, "but I'm worried about my brother. He's very sick and the doctors don't seem to be able to help him. I wonder if I could get you to do me a favor."

"Sure," I said, "if it is possible. What would you like me to do?"

"My brother is in a nearby hospital and he is on the critical list. Would you stop in and work on him?"

"I think that can be arranged. What's wrong with him anyway?"

Sally hesitated. "Well," she said, "he's HIV positive and now he has cancer. He's bleeding internally and the doctors can't find the source of the bleeding. The loss of blood is making him very weak."

"Okay, I'll arrange to stop by and see him during visiting hours. By the way, do you know when visiting hours are?"

"Yes," said Sally, "they're in the early evening."

"That'll work out fine," I said. "I can go over there tomorrow after I get finished here at the center."

"That would be great. I really appreciate your help in this matter," she said.

The next evening I went to the hospital. When I entered the room, I saw a big lanky guy lying in bed. He was so tall that his feet extended over the end of the bed.

"Hello there," I said, entering his room.

"Hello," he said. "Are you one of the 'wolf pack'?"

"The 'wolf pack'?" I responded, confused.

"Yeah, you know, one of the doctors. They usually come to see me in a group, so I've nicknamed them the 'wolf pack.'"

"Oh," I said. "Well, I'm afraid I'm going to have to disappoint you. I'm not a doctor. My name is Gene Egidio, I'm a healer. Your sister asked me to come over and take a look at you."

"I'm Bob," he said, as he extended his hand to me.

"Sally tells me you are on the critical list and are bleeding internally."

"Yes, that's right, and the worst thing is the doctors can't find the cause of the bleeding. I really appreciate your coming to see me, but there seems to be nothing anyone can do."

"How do they know you're bleeding?" I asked.

"There's physical evidence: I have a very bad case of diarrhea that's unstoppable and blood is the main content."

As I stood there looking at him, I suddenly received an insight that seemed rather strange. "I know this is going to sound funny, but I am receiving the thought that you should be drinking three cans of Coca-Cola every day for a while."

Bob's eyebrows shot up in a quizzical look. "Yeah, you're right. That does sound strange, but at this point I'm willing to try anything, so I'll do it."

I knew I needed to work with him for a while and I set up

a phone appointment with him for the next evening. He kept the appointment and we did some work on the phone.

"Well," Bob said, "I've drunk six cans of Coca-Cola since I saw you. The diarrhea has stopped, but the bleeding hasn't."

"Okay," I said, "I want you to close your eyes. We're going to take a journey through your body. Let's start at your feet. Look at your feet and tell me what you see in your mind's eye."

"My feet are fine," he responded.

"Okay, let's start up your right leg."

"No problems there," Bob said, "and the left leg's okay too."

"Let's move into the abdominal area. What do you see there?"

"Nothing unusual."

"Okay, let's go to your chest area. Do you see anything out of the ordinary there?"

Bob paused, then said nervously, "I think I see something; it is a black spot."

"Well, get closer and see if you can see what the black spot is."

He was quiet for a moment and then he said, "Oh my God, there is a vein that is shooting blood out, and it's going everywhere! What should we do?"

Since I'd been an electrician, I said, "Let's tape it up. See the vein being taped, and make sure the tape is reinforced, so it doesn't break open again."

He was silent for a couple of minutes.

Finally I quietly asked, "Bob, have you finished taping the vein in your meditation?"

"Yes," he said, "I've got it now."

"Okay, let's continue on with our journey through your body to make sure there are no other problems."

Finally we reached the top of his head, and he had found no other problems.

"Bob, you did some really good work today. Now I want you to get a good night's rest and we'll do some more work tomorrow."

"Okay," he answered. "As a matter of fact, I'm very tired."

The next night at six sharp, the phone rang and it was Bob.

"You won't believe this," he said happily, "but the bleeding has stopped. What's more, the 'wolf pack' was here earlier and when they saw all the Coca-Cola cans, one of the doctors commented that Coca-Cola was a good way to stop diarrhea."

"Well, it sounds as if you are on your way to recovering your health," I said.

"Yes, and there is more good news. The 'wolf pack' told me that since the bleeding has stopped, I have a good chance of being discharged in two or three days."

"I like the sound of that. You keep up the good work now," I said to Bob as I hung up the phone.

A week went by and I got another call from Bob.

"So, how's everything by you?" I asked him when I heard his voice on the other end of the phone.

"Fine, fine, couldn't be better," he replied. "I have been out of the hospital for four days and this morning I bought a motor home. I've decided that I am going to travel across the country and see the United States and just enjoy myself."

"Sounds like a good choice," I said. "I hope you have a good time."

Bob's desire to take another look at life played a major role in his being able to overcome the health problems he was facing, and the mental visualizing he did was a tool that served him well.

In laymen's terms, the mind is sometimes referred to as man's thinking muscle, and what Bob was able to accomplish just substantiates what I always say: "The mind is the strongest muscle in the body."

Bob was able to find the source of the bleeding and stop it with his mind, and a little help from the "guy upstairs."

Life Insurance

Many times after people have had successful healings with me, they return for a checkup and at that time they are usually interested in information on keeping their good health. One woman with this interest was Julie, who came to me complaining of migraine headaches. After two or three sessions the headaches disappeared, and I didn't see her for a while. After a few months, she called and said she wanted another healing.

"Okay, I'll have my assistant make an appointment," I told her.

At the end of her session, she said, "Gene, how can I stay strong and healthy?"

"Look outside, Julie. Pick one of the trees in my yard and look at it."

She looked at the trees for a couple of seconds, then said, "Okay, I'm going to pick that middle one, because I like its shape."

"Fine. Now, what do you notice about the tree?"

"Its leaves are green."

"True, but the important thing to notice is that it has its roots firmly planted, and it's receiving nutrients from the earth that give it the strength to stand up straight."

"Okay, I'll buy that."

"But even though its roots are firmly planted, as you go up the trunk to the branches, you can see that they're capable of bending when they encounter winds. Even though the trunk is connected to roots that keep it firmly planted, it can still bend when necessary."

"Yes."

"Not unlike ourselves, Julie. We need to plant ourselves firmly into the spiritual laws that govern this planet so that when man's law comes at us we'll be able to bend with it. Like ourselves, the tree takes its nourishment from the heavens; it receives the rains and the sun and creates lovely branches and leaves. As time passes it relinquishes the leaves that do not service it anymore. We too must relinquish old habits and old ways that do not work for us anymore, and always be willing to embrace new ways."

"That's a beautiful story," said Julie.

"Wait, I'm not finished," I said, smiling at her. "Even in death the tree lives on. It creates fuel for us to us to warm ourselves, or paper for us to write our stories. So we must always keep a strong and firm root, but yet we must remain flexible. This is the way to stay young at heart and strong in mind."

Don't Tell Granddad

Not everyone I run into *wants* to be healed. As a matter of fact, there are times when people avoid me in order *not* to be healed. A case in point is what happened with my grandson.

One morning my daughter Annie went to wake up her son so he could get ready for school. As she glanced at him she noticed he had red blotches on his face. She felt his forehead and realized he was slightly feverish.

"Well, Anthony, I guess you won't be going to school today," she told him. "I think you have a fever, and in case you haven't looked into the mirror lately, you have red blotches all over your face."

"Really?" Anthony jumped out of bed and headed for the mirror.

"Really," said his mother. "I think you are coming down with a case of chicken pox, and it is a contagious disease, so you'll have to stay away from other people until we know for sure what the problem is."

As Anthony crawled back into bed, a big smile started spreading across his face from ear to ear.

"Well, I don't mind staying at home," he said happily.

"I guess I had better call a doctor and see if I can get an appointment for you to be checked out," Annie said, as she started to leave Anthony's room.

Suddenly Anthony got an alarmed look on his face and

said, "Mom, whatever you do, don't call Granddad and tell him I'm sick or he'll heal me and then I'll have to go to school!"

Sandy and the Chocolate Chip Cookie

Sometimes people come to me who consciously say they don't want to be healed, but their higher self has a different idea, and although they try on the physical level to avoid the healing, on another level they want it and eventually let the healing take place. I was put in touch with one such case one morning when I received a call from a lady, Irma, who said her daughter, Sandy, had a brain tumor.

"Is there any way you can help Sandy?" she asked anxiously.

"Well, that depends on her, of course, but we can always try," I answered.

"She is only seven and she's been traumatized by the many tests and doctors she's seen." Irma drew a breath and continued. "So if she reacts badly towards you don't be surprised. She really doesn't want to see any more doctors."

"Okay, I'll make an appointment for you, and we'll see what happens."

When she showed up for her appointment I was in the healing room working on a client. In those days I only worked on one person at a time and stressed a "no noise level" so my clients could go into a subliminal state. Suddenly I heard this loud shout coming from the living room. My client's eyes fluttered open, and I knew his subliminal state had been disturbed.

I hurried out to see what the problem was, and there was Sandy lying in the middle of the living room floor kicking and screaming. I looked at Irma. Her expression told me there was nothing she could do with her. By this time Sandy's squirming had gotten her close enough to some of my other clients that she was kicking at them.

"Whoa, whoa, you've got to stop kicking these people," I said to her.

Paying no attention to me, she continued to scream.

"I know she's a problem, but I would like for you to see her," Irma said.

I motioned for Irma to bring her into the healing room.

"Sandy, get up and come with me. We are going to go into another room," her mother said.

When Sandy heard the word "go," she was off the floor in a flash.

Her mother took her by the hand and led her into the healing room.

"I wonder if I could get you to sit on this chair," I said to her.

Sandy stood glued to the floor, staring at me.

"Would you like to sit in this chair?" I asked her.

She shook her head adamantly to let me know that nothing I could say would persuade her to sit on the recliner.

Then her mother tried. "Sandy, we have come all the way to see this man. If you don't let him work on you, we'll be seeing more doctors."

She held her ground. Nothing would persuade her to go near the chair.

Finally I said to her mother, "Irma, why don't you sit in the chair and hold her on your lap."

"Come on, Sandy," her mother said, "I am going to sit down and I want you to sit with me."

When her mother sat down and motioned for the child to sit on her lap, Sandy moved from the spot she had stood glued to from the moment she entered the room. Slowly she walked over to her mother and sat on her lap.

When I tried to get near her, she'd start screaming, and after several unsuccessful attempts to put my hand on her head, I saw the futility of it and ended up putting my hand on her mother's neck. Since Irma was holding Sandy I knew she would get some of my energy, even though it was going to be secondhand.

Finally Sandy went into a subliminal state; she started to doze off and I was finally able to put my hand on her head. I worked on the child for forty-five minutes and when she woke up she started screaming again.

"Look what I have for you," I said, handing her a crystal.

She eyed the crystal a moment, then she jumped off her mother's lap, snatched the crystal out of my hand, and went running out of the healing room.

"I'm so sorry," her mother said, looking at me helplessly.

"Don't worry about the outburst," I said. "She's been traumatized and she knows she's sick. That's enough to make the best of us difficult. Wait awhile and see how she is."

Late that evening the phone rang, and when I picked it up, it was Sandy's mother.

"I would like to bring Sandy back tomorrow," she said.

"Well, how is she?" I asked.

"She is quieter than she's been for a long time and hasn't complained about a headache at all today."

"Okay," I said, "we'll do it during my lunch break, so she won't disturb anyone if she has another outburst."

The next morning my doorbell rang promptly at 11:45 A.M. When I opened it, there stood Sandy. She had a ribbon in her hair and a lunch pail in her hand. She didn't bother to look at me—she just walked past me into the living room, headed straight for the healing room, and sat down on the recliner chair.

I followed her and when I saw her sitting on the chair, I looked at her mother in surprise. She too was surprised.

I sat down next to her. "How do you feel today?" I asked.

No answer. She leaned back on the recliner.

"Is it okay if I touch your head?" I asked.

Again no answer. She looked up at me and closed her eyes.

I'd better work on her before she changes her mind, I thought to myself and I worked on her for an hour.

When Sandy awoke I asked her mom to come into the healing room, and she made no attempt to get out of the chair.

As she sat there looking at us, I asked her, "Sandy, what did you feel in your head while I was working on you?"

She said nothing. Her mother asked the same question.

"I was cold," she answered abruptly.

"Well, can I put my hand on your head now?" I asked.

Sandy didn't move as I gently placed my hand on her head. "Does your head feel cold now?"

She nodded.

I knew we had taken care of her problem when she told me she was cold. It was just an intuitive knowing, but I knew she wouldn't have to be operated on.

I sat there with my hand on her head and she was very quiet. Then without a word she opened her lunch pail and pulled out a big cookie. As I watched, she measured it, then broke it and handed me one of the halves.

That was a nice gesture and it gave me a nice feeling knowing that she wanted to share her lunch with me.

"Well, thank you," I said, and I ate the cookie as I continued working on her head.

"Would you like to come back tomorrow?" I asked.

She nodded again.

"Sandy asked to eat food last night," Irma said. "Up until yesterday she was refusing everything. That crystal you gave her was a big hit. She wouldn't let anyone touch it and wouldn't put it down for a second. She even took it into her bath with her."

"Bring her back tomorrow. I'll give her a chain so she can wear the crystal around her neck."

The next day she arrived again promptly at 11:45 A.M. with her lunch pail, and we again went through the process of sharing a cookie.

"I don't usually do this, but I feel that she really needs a session tomorrow. I know it's Sunday, but would you be willing to bring her over?" I asked Irma.

Before her mother could get her mouth open, Sandy gave out a loud, resounding, "Yes!"

She showed up Sunday with a large chocolate chip cookie, and after I had worked on her, we shared it. Sandy knew she was getting better and I like to think that her willingness to share her lunch with me was her way of saying "Thank you."

When we finished the session and cookie, I told Irma that I thought the kid was going to be okay.

"Take her to your medical doctor and let him check her now," I said.

About a week later the phone rang. It was Irma. "Well, you were right," she said. "I took Sandy to the doctor and she got a clean bill of health. They could find no trace of the tumor, and best of all, she's eating and not complaining about headaches or blurred eyesight anymore, and she doesn't bump into things anymore, either."

"Good, I'm very happy for her."

Nearly a decade and a half went by and I happened to run into someone who knew Sandy.

"How is she?" I asked.

"Oh, she's fine," my friend said. "She's married and happy and living a full life."

"I'm glad! You know, that is the kind of ending I like to hear about."

The Voodoo Master

A few summers ago I had an offer to participate in a healing conference that was to be held on the beautiful island of Barbados. When I got there, the organizer who had invited me had arranged for me to stay in a cottage on the beach. The setting was picture perfect, with the blue sky meeting the transparent blue water, in what looked like an infinity of peaceful calmness.

After spending a relaxing evening, I was ready for the business meeting the next morning. This was the meeting that told everyone where their assigned spaces were and when they would be speaking at the healing conference.

When the speaker finished calling all the names, mine wasn't among them, and I wanted to find out why I'd been overlooked.

"I'd like to introduce myself. I'm Gene Egidio, and I didn't hear my name called. Was this an oversight?"

"Oh, no," the speaker assured me, "you haven't been given a place to do healings because the people on this island don't like what you do. As a matter of fact, I suspect they may feel threatened by you."

"But why?" I asked. "You saw me work yesterday, and everyone I worked on responded positively."

"True," he said, "and that's exactly why the powers that be on this island don't want you here."

"They don't like to see people improve their health?" I asked, dismayed.

"It's more than that."

"What do you mean?" I asked. "Just what don't they like?"

"They are superstitious in their ways and they feel that the fact that you use just your hands is reason enough to keep you from working on people here; you're not like them. If you were, you would use relics and other objects like they do."

"I was personally invited to take part in this conference, and I've spent a lot of money coming here, not to mention the rearrangement of my work schedule, and I want the space I was promised."

I could tell by the expression on his face, not to mention his apparent discomfort about what he had been instructed to tell me, that I was wearing him down. As I stood looking at him, he threw his hands in the air in a gesture of exasperation.

"Okay, okay, I'll see if I can get you a place to do your work, but you will not be permitted to speak at the conference, and that's final."

"Small difference," I mumbled. I knew that whether I was doing healings or speaking to a group, I would be healing, for people had only to be in my presence to start receiving the healing energy.

After conferring with a few people, he motioned me over to his table.

"I have a space for you to work," he said.

"Great!" I answered. "I knew you'd come through."

He shot me a look of dazed disbelief, but I continued to smile at him.

"So where's my space going to be?"

"Over there." He pointed to the hotel disco. "That's the space you've been assigned."

"You want me to do healings in a disco!"

"Take it or leave it," he snapped.

"Fine, I'll take it and tell them to leave the strobe lights on; it might put some jazz into my healings," I said, and I walked away.

Some of the other participants in the conference knew me, and one woman, Valerie Hunt, who had overheard the difficulty I was having, approached me. Valerie is a scientist/mystic, as well as a clinician/philosopher and a healer in her own right. She received international recognition from the scientific community for her pioneering research into human energy fields. She was the first to discover the subtle variances in our vibration patterns when we are in good health and then become sick, and she found a way to measure the subtle energetic happenings between people, therefore making it possible to present them as hard scientific evidence. After years of research and work she collected all this evidence and information and wrote about it in a book titled *Infinite Mind*. I had met her in California and I was impressed with her work, so I was happy to see her here.

"Gene, I couldn't help but overhear what the man said to you," Valerie said.

"Yeah, he's not exactly giving me a warm welcome."

"Don't worry, you can speak in my space and do your workshop there," she said, smiling.

"Okay. I really appreciate your offer, and I may take you up on it."

As the day wore on, we got our booths set up and put everything together so we could begin our work early the next morning.

When I went to open up the disco there were a lot of people waiting to see me.

One lady stands out vividly in my mind. She had a tumor protruding from her stomach. As I worked on her, I felt good about her healing. When I finished, she thanked me and as she started toward the door she happened to glance down at her stomach and saw there was no longer a protrusion. She started screaming and ran out of the disco.

After a long day that went rather well, I had dinner and retired for the evening.

The next morning I saw a circle of people standing far away from the disco door. As I walked toward the entrance, I happened to look down and there, lying scattered across the walk, were some miniature bones.

"What are these bones for?" I asked.

A man in the crowd said, "It is voodoo. The high priest does not want you here."

"Well, I'm sorry he feels that way," I said, and I started toward the door.

"No, no!" the man screamed. "Don't walk over the bones. If you do, you will die."

I looked at the frightened crowd, then bent down and scooped the bones up in my hands. The sound of a collective gasp was heard as the crowd stood watching.

"Now," I said, "where is this high priest or witch doctor or whatever he thinks he is?" A few members of the crowd pointed toward the check-in desk of the hotel.

"The desk clerk?" I asked incredulously.

"No, the head bellboy. He is the most powerful high priest this island has had in a long time. Don't cross him or bad things will happen to you."

"We'll just see about that," I said, and I marched across the lobby to the bellboy/priest. He was smiling venomously at me. When I dumped the bones onto the counter the smile faded and his face twisted with rage and anger.

"Are these bones yours?" I asked.

He stared at me but said nothing.

"Don't put those bones across my door again. If you do, I'll not only bring them back to you, but I'll make you eat them."

I turned and walked out of the hotel. The crowd was still at the disco, waiting to see the result of the encounter.

I opened the door and announced, "As you can see, I'm all right. Nothing's happened to me."

They continued to stare in silence.

"I'd like to invite you in to share and enjoy my healing energy," I said with a smile. With a cheer they started moving toward the door.

I continued doing healings in the disco for the rest of my time on the magical island and never had another problem with the bellboy/high priest.

He'd apparently decided that my healing energy was stronger than his voodoo, and he gave me a cordial greeting whenever we ran into each other.

The Guru

One afternoon in my Santa Monica center, I had an over-
load of people, as well as some animals — a dog, a cat, a ger-
bil, and a parrot. As I was passing my hand over the dog
lying on the living room couch, I glanced out the window,
and I saw a group of people in orange robes coming up the
walk.

I held the screen door open, and said, "I'm sorry, but the
center is full today."

One of the men came forward and said, "That's okay, we
don't mind sitting on the lawn."

"Fine," I said, "I'll see you as soon as I can."

When I finished with the animals I went outside. There
were about fifteen disciples with their guru sitting in the
center of a circle they formed around him. The man I had
spoken to came forward and introduced himself.

"I am the business manager for this very revered guru,"
he said, extending his hand.

"Nice to meet you. What can I do for you?"

"It's not me, it's my master. He would like for you to see
if you can help him with a health problem he's developed."

The guru was in a lotus position as I held my hands a few
inches from his heart and crown chakras. After a few minutes he nodded and gestured that he felt better. He was not
speaking English. He whispered something to his business

manager, then marched off with his followers. The manager looked after them, then turned to me.

"Thank you," he said. "The master is satisfied with your help."

"Glad to be of service," I answered.

I dismissed the incident and went back to the menagerie that was waiting in my office.

About two months later I got a call from the manager. "Please come to the guru's house tonight," he said. "My master would like you to dine with him. I will give you the address and we'll expect to see you at 7 P.M. His house is on the very top of a mountain in Beverly Hills."

"Okay," I replied, then thought, Well, after all, I did provide the cheapskate with a service, and he didn't even bother with so much as a dog's donation. Besides, I like Indian food. Maybe he'll make up for it with a great Indian dinner at the top of his mountain. At six, I put on a clean shirt and off I went to Beverly Hills.

It was the middle of July and hot. As soon as the manager answered the door I asked for something cold to drink. He brought me a giant glass of ice water and proceeded to lead me through a maze of hallways and rooms until we reached the guru's apartment. The place was so magnificent that I found myself becoming uncomfortable.

The guru was entertaining a roomful of followers. When I entered, he motioned them away and waved me onto a beautiful white velvet couch. As I walked through the thick carpet toward him, I tripped and spilled the water onto the white velvet.

I was embarrassed and, trying to keep it light, said, "There won't be any charge for the blessing of the couch." Nothing. Not a smile, not a blink of the eye. I spoke slowly, as I might to a child or an idiot. "If you'll send for your business manager he'll interpret and we can talk."

"I speak English," the guru said, eyeing me closely.

"Well then, why didn't you speak to me when you were at my place?"

"I didn't feel the need to do so." He paused for effect, then said, "I'd like to show you something." With that, he opened an attaché case filled to the brim with hundred-dollar bills.

I looked at it and thought, Well, Egidio, this isn't quite the curry dinner you'd anticipated, is it? That much money was instant heartburn to a healer fighting his way out of poverty.

"You can take your first month's salary from here," he said.

"Really? I don't understand."

"Just reach in and take a handful of bills."

"For what?"

"I want you to be my private healer."

"I can't be your private healer," I said. "I'm here for everyone, not just a handful of people. I can't work exclusively for you or anyone else; that's not what my mission is about, but I'll gladly take a fistful of bills out of your attaché case, if you want."

This angered him, and with a point of his finger I received the classic child's punishment: "If you won't be my private healer, I don't want you here. Leave now!"

"But I haven't had dinner," I said with a touch of humor that went completely over his head.

"Go!" he said and rang for his business manager, who quickly escorted me back through the maze until we reached a large dining room.

"Wait here until dinner is served," he said, then turned and left.

Oh boy, I thought to myself, this is interesting and a lot of fun, but dinner had better be good! And it was. The room was elegant and so was the table. After a short wait the guests entered and I enjoyed one of the best curries I've ever tasted. When dinner was finished the manager escorted me to the front door.

"Well, I bid you a good night," I said, with what I thought was an elegant Oriental bow. "I'm sorry I couldn't give your guru what he wanted, but my mission's been laid out for me and I have to follow it."

He bowed back and closed the door.

Well, that's the end of that, I thought, but oddly enough, our paths did cross again.

A few years later, as I was struggling with customs at the Moscow airport, I happened to glance up and saw a man whom I recognized as the guru's business manager rushing toward me.

"My guru's plane is sitting on the runway waiting for clearance to take off for India," he said breathlessly. "He's willing to forget about what happened in Beverly Hills and give you another chance to reconsider his offer. Just get on the plane, and we'll get your belongings through customs."

I considered it for a moment, but I knew I had a different agenda. "I'm flattered. I really am, but tell your master I'm declining his offer again. Serving him is not the thing I am supposed to be doing." I closed the conversation with my Oriental bow. "Please, give your guru my best regards."

The man eyed me for a moment, returned the bow, and left as quickly as he had appeared. When my eyes went back to the mean Russian customs guy, I was smiling. When you do the right thing, even red tape can feel good.

The Art of Manifesting

Many people are interested in learning how to manifest the things they want in their lives. In Open Eye Meditation, we practice "learning to manifest" by using the master mind principle. The master mind is another word for whatever you call God.

The purpose of participating in a master mind group is to establish a conscious contact with the Universal Spirit. For members to experience an increased awareness and power, they must be made aware of the master mind working through them. A master mind meeting is not designed to solve our problems, but to turn the perspective of problems around, to heal, or just to develop the consciousness of the master mind.

Betty was a charming woman who could manifest anything for anyone but herself. She showed up for class one day and said, "Gene, I'm in trouble. I really need a job."

I was elated when she said that, at last, she was going to ask for something for herself. "Put it out to the universe," I told her, and she shouted, "God, I need a job!"

The next time Betty came to class, she said, "Gene, I've got the job, but now I need a car to get there."

"Go to it," I said. "You know what to do."

A week later she pulled up in a red Mazda.

What Betty had succeeded in "manifesting" in two short

weeks was amazing. "Hey, kid," I said, "you should be proud of yourself. You pulled it off."

"You don't know the half of it, Gene," she said. "After I got the job and car, my boyfriend, who moved to Africa, proposed to me the other night and wants me to move to Africa." She paused, beaming.

"I'm going to do it, Gene. I love this guy and I'm going to marry him."

"Wonderful!" I said, and suddenly she became secretive.

"Look, Gene, I know that you can go places while you're in a dream state. I'll be in Africa for the next few years. I'll be lonely. If you can make it, drop by some night and visit us."

Six months later I got a letter from her.

The letter began,

Dear Gene,

My husband and I want to thank you for dropping by and visiting us. You have definitely made my husband a believer, because we both saw you when you dropped in.

Hope to see you again soon.

Betty

The Deep South

One day as I was working in my center the phone rang. After a few exchanges of dialogue, my assistant, Barbara, informed me there was someone who needed to talk to me.

"Hello," I said. "What can I do to help you?"

"My name is Kim and my mother is very ill," she said.

"Would you like an appointment?" I asked.

"Well, that's just it. My mother is too ill to travel, and my brothers and I were wondering if you would consider coming here to work on her."

"I don't usually do that," I replied. "Just where is it you are located?"

"We live in the South," she responded, "and I know there are many people here who would also love to have you work on them. If you'll consider coming here to work on my mother, we'll organize these people for you to make your coming worthwhile."

I was dubious, but I could hear the need in her voice so I said, "Well, I guess that could be arranged; the only thing I need is a plane ticket, and enough money to offset the expenses I am leaving here at my center."

"That's not a problem; we'll put something together for you," she assured me.

"Okay, why don't we set a date three months from now. That should give you enough time to organize my stay. Let's shoot for the first two weeks in June."

"We'll put it together," Kim said.

April came and went and May came and went and there was no plane ticket. I was starting to lose faith, but Kim was still calling me periodically, telling me she and her family were still working out the details, so I went along with her.

"You know, it is the middle of May, what's happening with the plane ticket?" I inquired during one of her many phone calls.

"Rest assured that everything will be okay, you'll see," she replied.

The more I thought about it, the more I knew I needed to be there. I also knew there was not going to be a plane ticket.

One day during the last week of May the phone rang; it was Kim. "Listen," she said, "just buy the ticket, and we'll reimburse you when you get here."

I instinctively knew that wasn't going to happen, but I bought the plane ticket, and after a long day of traveling, and changing planes three times, I wound up in a tiny airport in the middle of nowhere.

When I got off the plane I looked around; there was no one there to meet me. Since I didn't have much choice, I decided to stick around for a while to see what might develop. Finally, after sitting around in a totally deserted airport for an hour or more, I glanced up and I saw two people dressed in flowing, brightly colored African attire approaching.

Oh, I guess I haven't been forgotten after all, I thought to myself.

When Kim reached me, she extended her hand. "Hello, I'm Kim, and this is my brother."

"Nice to meet you," I said. "For a minute there, I thought maybe you had forgotten about my arrival."

"No, no," she said, without bothering to apologize for being late. "We've set aside a room in our house especially for you, and we're all set."

"Good."

"Tomorrow we have arranged for you to meet with a minister friend of ours, and the next day you'll be meeting with the minister of one of our local churches."

"This may not work out very well," I said, scratching my head. "You see, I don't subscribe to any religion, and as a general rule church members don't welcome someone into their midst unless they're of the same faith."

"Things will be different here," they assured me. "These people will welcome you. In fact, we have a minister waiting for you at our house. He is the pastor of a large Protestant church here."

"Well, I'll be surprised if he accepts me," I reiterated.

When we reached their home, the minister and his wife were sitting in the living room. I walked over and extended my hand.

"Hi, I'm Gene Egidio," I said.

He gave me a cold stare and didn't take my hand.

"What religious denomination are you?" he said.

"I don't really bring religion into my healing," I said lightly.

"Well, if you are not from my church, you're not going to pray over me and I forbid you to see any of my people."

He did not use the word "heal"; instead, he said again adamantly, "I don't want you praying over my people." With that, he grabbed his wife by the hand and made toward the door.

I'd been traveling all day. I was very tired and was interested in getting some much-needed rest, but I couldn't resist saying, "If you want to get rid of that pain in your chest, come back and see me."

He was halfway out the door when he turned and exclaimed, "How'd you know I had a pain in my chest? That's surely proof that you must be in cahoots with the devil!"

He hurriedly bustled his wife out of the room, and the poor people who had invited me were very upset.

"Well, I think this is what will happen with all the ministers you have lined up for me to meet," I told Kim and her brother. "But don't be too concerned, your friend'll be back as soon as he's taken his wife home. He wants to have a healing with me, but doesn't want anyone to see that he's allowed me to work on him."

"I don't think so," said Kim. "He seemed pretty definite about not letting you near him or any members of his congregation."

"Just wait," I said.

An hour had passed when there was a knock on the door.

"It's midnight. Who'd come to see us this late?" Kim asked.

"Well, let's open the door and find out," I said as I walked to the door.

The minister entered the room, stood in front of me, and said, "I've decided that I will be the guinea pig for my people. I am going to let you work on me."

"Okay, let's go in the other room. I want you to lie down here on the bed." He complied. I worked on him for a few minutes and he dozed off. I later found out that he was sleeping in my bed, and I had to wait for him to wake up.

After about an hour and a half, he woke up and came back into the living room.

"Okay, now please tell these people whether you still have a pain in your chest or not," I said, looking him straight in the eye.

"No, it's gone. Thank God it's gone."

"I'm very happy for you," I said. "Now I must say goodnight; I really need some rest." With that I headed to the room that had been set aside for me.

It was a hot, sultry, humid night, there was no air conditioning, and I had the window open as wide as possible. I got undressed and was stark naked when I dropped off into a deep sleep. Within minutes a bright light woke me. I had the idea that this was a miracle, a sign of someone with great powers descending. I was disoriented and blinked frantically trying to get a grip on my reality. I sat up and saw that the miracle was the overhead ceiling lamp shining into my eyes. I was hot and tired, and rasped, "Who turned those bloody lights on in the middle of the night?"

There was no response. There I was stark naked on the bed with no cover and nowhere to hide when I turned and saw three people kneeling beside my bed praying. That was a jolt. Believe me when I say it took me more than just a moment to pull myself together.

At this point I wasn't sure just what their motives were for asking me there. Their customs were very different from anything I had been exposed to up to that point. I was beginning to wonder if I might not wind up on the menu as breakfast.

I looked at them with their heads bowed and asked, "What's the problem? Why are you kneeling around my bed?"

"Oh, there's no problem," Kim replied. "It is time for our morning prayers and we want you to lead them."

"Okay," I said, "God bless our home. Now let me get some sleep."

"No," Kim said, "you have to get out of bed and kneel too before you can pray."

I wanted this invasion of my privacy to end and I knew the only way it would was if I complied with their request, so I pulled a sheet around me, got out of bed, and kneeled beside them. I blessed everything and everyone, and whatever I said must have satisfied them, because they got up and started leaving the room.

"What time is it?" I asked.

"Five-thirty. We always get up when the sun rises."

"Well, I am going to sleep a little longer."

"Okay," Kim said.

I got up and turned the light off and got back in bed. I no sooner fell asleep than bang! The room was flooded with that bright light again.

They all three came in and Kim said, "Breakfast is ready."

I saw there was going to be no chance of getting any more sleep, so I begrudgingly got out of bed, got dressed, and joined them at the breakfast table. After breakfast I asked them what was on the agenda for the day.

Kim smiled. "We are going to try to get some people together for you to work on here," she said.

"What, you mean you don't have them together already?" I asked, dismayed.

"No."

"But why? You said you were going to have lots of people for me to work on."

"We couldn't get them together because our phone isn't working."

"What is wrong with your phone?" I asked.

"Oh, it just isn't working."

After prodding and prying for a considerable length of time, I finally found out that the phone wasn't working because they hadn't paid the bill.

Of course, I paid it.

Later that morning Kim had a C.O.D. package come in from Africa; it was a shipment of herbs. They made their living by mixing and selling various herbal combinations for medicinal purposes. I ended up paying for that too. So far the trip was running about eight hundred dollars out of my pocket. I was not so disturbed about the money part as the fact she didn't have anything arranged for me; there were no people for me to work on. She had made all those promises to me just to get me to come and work on her mother. I didn't get angry about this, but I did try to talk to her.

"You know, Kim, what you did really wasn't right. You made promises you had no intention of keeping, and you did that just to get me here to work on your mother. You deceived me, and that is not a good way for one human to treat another."

"Okay, now that the phone is working, I will see if I can get some people together," she said at last.

She spent the morning calling people, and she did succeed in getting some people to come over. Even though there were not many people, we got some very good results with those who did come. Then she suggested we go to another more rural town where she knew some people. These were people whose ancestors had been brought to this country as slaves. Even though they were far removed from slavery, I was struck by the immense amount of control leaders, and especially the religious leaders of the community, had over these poor folks.

I remember one lady in particular who came to me for healing. After an hour or so had passed her energy field looked very good, and her physical appearance was radiant.

In passing, I said, "Well, it looks like you are ready to go out dancing tonight."

"I only dance with the Lord," she said.

"Well, you picked the best partner," I replied. "How do you feel?"

"Not so good," she responded.

"What's wrong?" I asked.

"I have cancer."

I couldn't understand, because as I looked at her I couldn't feel that vibration in her body, and I couldn't understand why it wasn't showing up. "When were you diagnosed?" I asked.

"Oh, I wasn't diagnosed by a medical doctor."

"Then how do you know you have cancer?"

"The minister of my church said I had cancer because I sinned."

I was speechless. Finally I asked, "Well, how long have you known about this?"

"Oh, he told me about this three years ago, after I had done something he said God wouldn't like."

"I see," I said. I thought to myself, Can you imagine living with something like that, and worse still, can you imagine the kind of person who'd say something like that to another person.

I got very disturbed over that, and I asked my organizers to arrange a meeting with this minister. They knew I was upset and would not let me meet him, so I decided to have a long talk with this woman.

"You know, the power that your minister took away from you belongs to you and you alone, and I think you should take it back. You are a healthy vibrant woman, and you shouldn't believe these negative things that were said. First of all, it's not true, and second, it was said to you as a means of gaining control over you."

I spent three days in that town and I was amazed at how backward it was. I ran into people who believed they should punish their children in severe and harsh ways because they had behaved in such a way as to imply they might not believe in God. It was very disheartening.

By the last two days of my stay the word had gotten around, and fifty people showed up at this little apartment. On the last day I had people sitting on chairs, beds, couches, and the floor. As I was making the rounds, a group of five people came in with their Bibles open, and as I worked they followed me and prayed to the Lord that I would be saved. They let it be known that they thought I was doing the work of the devil.

So here we were in twentieth-century America, and it was like being transported back to the Middle Ages when witch hunts were popular. The consciousness in this rural area was very low, and until the time when something happens to make it possible for it to be raised, this kind of behavior will keep going on. I had intuitively known that I needed to go there, but I could not have begun to fathom what I would find until I saw it firsthand.

This was only one experience; there were many more stories and touching moments. There was a ten-year-old boy I worked on. He had a problem with his leg and was having trouble walking. After I worked on him he found he could walk without difficulty. He was so elated that he handed me two rolls of pennies and said, "I want to help you; I've been saving my pennies for a long time and I want you to have them. I would give you more, but this is all I have."

This was a beautiful and amazing gesture.

"Well, I want you to keep those pennies, and to build on them, so you will have funds for your education when you get older."

"Thank you," he said, "I'll do that."

At the end of my third day I was taken back to the airport. I left with no hard feelings and very empty pockets.

I guess this was another lesson for me. I really have no animosity toward people who harbor such beliefs, because we are all going to the same place; we just take different roads to get there, and sometimes some of the roads take longer than others. We are all here to facilitate each other with learning experiences.

I live in California, and the mass consciousness here is far higher than in that small rural community I had visited. If we choose to be a part of a mass consciousness that is more evolved, we have a better chance of getting to do what we want and an easier time achieving our goals.

The mass consciousness we choose to be a part of truly plays a large role in determining what happens to us in our lives. Naturally we always have the choice to do what we want to do in life. This is the spice I call free will, that gives us that open area to express ourselves, but the mass consciousness of the group we belong to is also an important influence.

During the seven days I stayed in this southern town I must have been confronted with seven or eight different belief systems, and as I was saying farewell to these people at the airport, I was saying to myself, What a relief! I thanked God that I was opening up the church within me and did not need to go to the marble, brick and mortar, or wooden structures built by man to practice my religion.

As I always say, we are all spiritual beings here on earth for a physical experience, not physical beings here for a spiritual experience.

In the short time I have been doing healing work I've been fortunate, for many spiritual beings have crossed my path. Some of the ones I admire extensively—Manny P. Hall, Billie Baker, Valerie Hunt, and J. Donald Walters—come to mind. These persons all had their consciousness within themselves and this set the stage for all of them to go out and do their work.

I Go to the Animal Hospital

Although I work extensively with people, I have had my share of animal healings too. I remember one night I was awakened from a deep sleep by the phone ringing. I looked at the clock. It was 3:30 A.M.

I thought to myself, Either this is a wrong number or someone has an emergency.

I answered the phone and heard the voice of a distraught woman crying so hard she could barely talk.

"I just took him to the hospital," she said, "and he is not expected to live. You've got to help me."

"Sure," I answered.

"I'll come by and pick you up in ten minutes and take you to the hospital."

Obligingly, I said, "Okay."

I jumped into my clothes and sure enough, about ten minutes later, a car pulled up to the curb and honked and we went speeding off in the direction of the hospital. All the time she was going on and on about how he was not expected to live.

"I don't know what to make of it," she said. "One minute he was fine and then wham! He was so sick he wouldn't even look at me when I tried to talk to him. And what's more he wouldn't eat. All this happened in the space of twenty-four hours. No warning, nothing!

"When I got him to the hospital the doctors said they didn't think he would make it through the night."

I wasn't sure what the problem was; she was too emotional to tell me, and I thought I'd just wait and see.

When we turned into the hospital driveway, I looked up and, to my surprise, I saw that it was an animal hospital. Her *dog* was sick.

I thought, Oh well, I am here, so I might as well do what I can. The result was a night spent working on a lot of dogs and cats. Her dog recovered and she was able to take him home the next day.

I usually take animals into my center, but when a couple called and wanted to bring in their sick snake, I said, "No!"

I have never liked snakes and I didn't want one in my center. The owners were so upset about my refusal to treat the sick snake that I finally agreed to do a photo healing on it.

As far as I know the snake recovered, because I never heard from the couple again.

I Heal the Plants

On one of my journeys to Leningrad (called St. Petersburg since 1991), I was asked to do a healing on some rare plants that were dying. These plants were housed in a grand greenhouse made of stone and glass that had been built in the 1850s. I'd never thought about healing a plant, but I knew that all living things have a life force, and so I agreed to see what I could do.

The Russians, I later learned, accepted the fact that there is a life force in plants because of the extensive work done by the Russian researcher Semyon Kirlian. He had been a pioneer in figuring out a way to photograph the energy fields, or auras, of plants.

"Are you familiar with Kirlian photography?" my interpreter asked me as we made our way to the greenhouse.

"Well, I've seen some of the photographs," I answered. "Did you know that the aura of a person becomes smaller when he is photographed after eating a greasy cheeseburger and french fries?"

"No, I didn't know that," she responded.

"And, by the same token, the aura of a person eating uncooked vegetables and fruits becomes larger when photographed. That sure says a lot about how our bodies respond to the food we choose to ingest, doesn't it?"

"Yes, I suppose it does. Actually, it's the same for plants. When they're sick their auras change. You know, Kirlian photography was begun right here in Russia in the 1940s and his work is still being expanded upon today."

"Well, that is very interesting," I responded politely. "Actually, all I know about Kirlian photography is that you have to have very special equipment."

"Yes, Semyon Kirlian made it possible for that equipment to be developed, but actually he started with a simple high-frequency electrographic apparatus. He connected it to an electrode beneath a sheet of film. The high-frequency current sent to the electrode created an electrical field on the photographic film, so when a grounded object, such as a finger, was placed on the film with a high electrical potential, there was a pathway created for the electrons of the highly charged electrical field to travel to the grounded object with a lower electrical potential. This caused a generation of sparks from the energy field of the object, and it was this that he tried to capture on film," she explained.

"Well, I could understand how that would work, for I know energy always flows from a high charge to a low charge. That is basically how my healing works."

"Yes, I can see how that might be," answered my interpreter, "but Kirlian went one step further. He had to have blind faith in what the seers of the time told him, for he'd never seen an aura himself and, since he was doing scientific research, he had to have a rational way to prove this life force that only a few people could see actually existed. After much pondering he settled on the theory of the corona around our sun, for that had been proven, and tried to adapt that to his photographic work. He knew as did other scientists that luminous bodies such as the sun and moon gave off concentric circles of light and this was named the corona discharge phenomenon.

"Kirlian decided that all living things must have luminous bodies, and therefore he reasoned that they too were giving off concentric circles of light, which we would call the aura,"

Maria continued. "It was this corona phenomenon that he attempted to capture on film. After he captured it, he was then ready to experiment with plants and people. He found out that the auras of sick people were drastically different from the auras of healthy people. He also found out that if a leaf was torn in half, the aura of the entire leaf was still present when it was photographed. It is because of his work that the ground has been laid for you to do today what you have been asked to do in order to help the plants."

"I sure am glad no one thinks this is a strange thing to do," I said, as we continued on our way to the greenhouse.

"The plants you are going to see are very exotic," she said.

"Are there any man-eating plants? I won't become their lunch if I try to heal them, will I?" I asked, jokingly.

She gave me an amused look. "Oh, I doubt very much if that could happen," she said. "This collection of plants came from every corner of the world. This greenhouse was built in the 1850s, which was when the collection was started. This greenhouse was the czar's pride and joy, and many brilliant scientific minds have spent hours inside these buildings learning about the characteristics of these plants."

"Is this the first time any of the plants have been sick?" I asked, on a more serious note.

"Yes, nobody knows what it is or where it came from."

"And they can find no cause of this virus?"

"No. The reason it's so important to keep these plants alive is because many of them are all but extinct, and it's the only record we have of the plant life that once existed so abundantly on this planet," she explained.

"Too bad," I said. "I find it impossible to understand why the people who make up the governments of countries the world over fail to understand the importance of taking care of the natural resources such as air and water and plant life. These are three things absolutely essential to our physical existence and we are slowly killing ourselves and everything on this planet for a few dollars of greedy profit. I hope we humans don't learn our lesson too late."

When we reached the greenhouse the driver stopped the car. Some of the staff came out, greeted us, and told us to follow them.

We went into a large and majestic courtyard. Off one side of the courtyard stood a row of glass greenhouses. In places they stood three stories tall. The architect who had envisioned these structures had definitely been from a time where no expense need be spared, but now as I looked at them I saw that about fifty percent of the glass panes were either broken or cracked, and as we stepped inside I saw a heating system that was probably unique for 1850, but this was the 1990s and they hadn't kept abreast of newer technology.

The heating system consisted of several gigantic belts on pulleys. These belts turned huge fans that hung from the ceilings, and the fans in turn circulated the hot air through the greenhouses. The fact that the environment was no longer intact was probably contributing to the vulnerability of the plants, but I wasn't there to discuss the upkeep of the place; I was there to do what I could to help the plants.

The local TV station thought it would add some color to the evening newscast and sent a crew to film the healing.

As we started going through the greenhouse one of the botanists would stop along the way and point to first one plant and then another. He would tell my interpreter what the problem was and she in turn would relay it to me. I worked on all the plants that needed special attention just as I would work on people, with a hands-on healing.

It took the entire morning, and by the time I'd finished I'd worked on hundreds of different plants, and the TV crew filmed the entire event. There was no way for me to tell when I left the greenhouse if my healings had been successful, but when I inquired about the health of the plants on a later trip, I was told they had all survived and were doing well. This incident brought home to me the realization that when an imbalance occurs on the planet, it is not only the people who are affected, but every living thing.

I Ace the Test

During my second trip to the Soviet Union I was introduced to Dr. Victor Slotsky. Dr. Slotsky had a clinic in Moscow where he worked with war veterans who were in emotional shock. His therapy consisted of a mixture of everyday medicine, a little psychiatry, and some plain common sense. As he was working primarily with the mind, he was a strong advocate of hands-on healing and was the head of the Association of Energy Healers.

The organizers of my Moscow trip thought it would be a feather in my cap to meet with this gentleman and compare notes, so I agreed to a meeting.

When we arrived at the doctor's office, I looked around and saw many photographs of him with well-known people from all over the world. As I stood looking at the collection of photographs, I thought that he was a very impressive figure, both in the photographs and in person. He stood approximately six-foot-five and had very broad shoulders and snow-white hair. He wore a white medical jacket that came to his knees and he had a very formal air about him.

"Come in and sit down," he said, extending his hand to me. "I know you are a healer from America, and I would like permission to test your energy level. I have devised a machine that can give off energy readings and I would like to put it to the test."

"Okay by me," I said, smiling at him. "Let's do it."

With that, one of his assistants placed a band that had wires attached to it around my forehead. Then he placed another band around my face between my nose and upper lip. This band also had wires attached.

Dr. Slotsky stood in front of me as his assistant read off numbers from the meters of this apparatus. Slotsky frowned, then adjusted the dials on his energy scope. As he did this, he kept looking at me.

"Am I supposed to be feeling something?" I asked.

"No, no, there will be no discomfort for you," he answered.

He kept adjusting the dials on his machine and looking at me.

As far as energy coming in or leaving, I couldn't feel anything happening. Finally Dr. Slotsky turned off the scope, came over, and took off the bands.

"Am I finished? Did I pass the test?" I asked casually.

He didn't say anything but instead put the palm of his hand toward my forehead and started backing across the room. When he got to the other side of the room he started smiling and then he applauded very loudly.

"What happened?" I asked.

He walked over to me. "Let me shake your hand. The energy you're working with is so strong that it went off the scope."

"Oh?"

"Yes," he said. "At first I thought there was something wrong with the scope, but then when I put my hand up to your forehead and started backing across the room, I could feel your energy field all the way across the room. You are a healer in the true sense of the word."

"Thank you," I said.

That endorsement made me feel very good, and I discovered as time passed that I had found a fast and true friend in Dr. Slotsky. Throughout the years we've stayed in touch with each other, and on my various trips to the Soviet Union I have, from time to time, worked with him at his clinic. On one of my trips we jointly worked with some men who were in shock from whatever trauma they experienced during the war in Afghanistan. Many of these men couldn't sleep and some were in such bad shape that with just the snap of a finger they'd hide in a corner of the room. We had some good successes in helping these men.

During one of my visits to the Soviet Union, Dr. Slotsky told me he had a client with a very special problem whom he would like me to see.

As always, I agreed to his request and he set up an appointment. Shortly after I arrived at his clinic, in walked a very young woman who was smartly dressed. She spoke English better than I, so it was no problem telling her about the procedure I wanted to go through with her.

When she got settled, I sent her energy and she immediately went into a subliminal state. About five minutes passed and I could see traces of perspiration on her face. I told Dr. Slotsky I wanted to see him outside, but that I wanted someone to watch her. He motioned for one of the nurses to come and stay with her.

"What is it you want to talk to me about?" asked Dr. Slotsky.

"Who is she and what is wrong with her?" I asked.

"Well, she is the daughter of a high Communist official and she has a virus in her body that no one can identify. That is all I can tell you."

"How did she get the virus?"

"No one knows, but she's getting very weak and continues to lose weight no matter how much she eats."

"Is she the only person with this virus?"

"Yes, as far as we know. She travels a great deal, so she might have picked something up while she was outside the country."

As I stood there pondering the situation, the nurse stuck her head into the room, with a rather alarmed expression on her face. "You had better come in and take a look at what's going on," she said.

Dr. Slotsky and I found the young woman drenched in perspiration. It looked as if someone had taken a bucket of water and poured it over her. Her blouse was so wet it clung to her skin.

"The virus is coming out," I said.

Dr. Slotsky nodded in agreement and we left her alone for another hour and a half. When she awoke I told the nurse to get her some dry clothes.

"How do you feel?" I asked, after she had changed.

"Very strange," she said. "I feel exhausted and I feel like I need to sleep forever."

"Don't sleep forever, but it would be a good idea for you to sleep when you get home," I told her.

The next day Dr. Slotsky called me and said the woman had called him that morning. She felt much better and was so hungry she was eating everything in sight.

The energy I sent her had triggered her body defenses into doing what needed to be done to rid her body of the virus.

It is always a pleasure to work with Dr. Slotsky. He's an outstanding person who has set standards on all levels for helping his fellow human beings and he has dedicated his life to this cause.

I Receive the Cosmonaut Medal

At an expo in Los Angeles I met Marina Popovich. Marina was an ex–test pilot from the U.S.S.R. Air Force and, I found out later, the first woman test pilot in Russia. She held the rank of colonel and, because of her rank, had become accustomed to the privileges that went with the territory. As we talked, I told her about my travels to Russia, and after listening awhile, she said she would like to invite me to the U.S.S.R. again, this time to visit the Cosmonaut Village. I thought about the invitation and it appealed to me, as I had always been interested in space travel.

After a couple months of correspondence, the trip was set into motion and back to Russia I went for yet another visit. As far as I know I was the first American allowed into this closed city. It was a frightening experience for me, for as we pulled up to the entrance gate in front of the village, the guards started questioning us after checking our identification. Marina was with me, and being the flamboyant person she was, she started screaming at the guards in Russian. She was very well known in the village—she made her home there—and within no time flat, the guards allowed us to enter.

We were taken to a very beautiful hotel that I would have to call deluxe, even by American standards. After we got our luggage to our rooms we were treated to a spectacular view of the village, as we were on one of the top floors. The village was surrounded by densely planted trees and below was a breathtaking promenade in the middle of a very carefully planned garden, somewhat like those of eighteenth-century Europe. The people who lived in this village were all well known in their fields and the government rewarded them by allowing them to have all the perks they could want. Their headquarters were exquisite; the grounds were beautiful; and they had access to excellent food, beautiful clothes, and the best cars. All in all it was a very plush, cushy life.

I was taken into an exhibit hall where I had my first meeting with some of the people who lived in the village. They were all very interested in what I did, and they kept asking me if I knew of some of the healers in the U.S.S.R. They dropped a lot of names, but none of them meant anything to me.

As we were going to the auditorium, where I was going to give a talk and do some healing demonstrations, a very unusual painting caught my eye. I stopped and turned to Marina. "I have never seen anything so exquisite. I must take a closer look."

"Fine. We've got time," she responded.

As I took a closer look at the painting, I saw that it was made completely of feathers, of all different colors and textures. It was spellbinding to look at. Luckily the artist who had done the paintings was there, and I got to talk to him.

"How did you ever come up with an idea to do feather paintings?" I asked him.

He smiled. "Well, there was a time when I couldn't afford to buy paint, so I started collecting feathers, and then the idea came to me that I could use the different colors of feathers in the same way as I would use the different colors of paint."

"Your work is very beautiful," I said.

"I must admit that it took a very long time to find all the different colors of feathers needed to create this piece."

"I can imagine," I told him.

At this point Marina came to tell me it was nearly time for me to speak, so I said good-bye to the artist and went into the auditorium.

When it was time for me to give my speech, I went on stage and told the people in the audience that I was here to support them in any way they needed, and I asked what I could do for them. During the course of my speech I used the word "love" several times, and I could see people turning their heads away and some of the women giggling. "Love" was apparently a word the Russians did not use in public. When I finished my speech, I did a quick healing on each of the fourteen hundred people present in the auditorium.

When the healing was over, I walked back on the stage with the intent of giving a short closing speech, but to my surprise Marina walked onto the stage. I hadn't expected her and wasn't sure how to proceed, but Marina didn't hesitate. She walked directly to center stage and announced to the audience that because of all the work I had done with the Russian people following the Chernobyl accident and the Armenian earthquake, she was going to present me with the Cosmonaut Medal. Everyone applauded.

I hadn't been informed of the plan, and I was dumbfounded. It was a very prestigious medal, and I was happy about having this honor bestowed upon me by the Russian people. This beautiful gold medallion had a picture of a cosmonaut embossed on it, and it is something that I shall treasure always.

After I recovered from the shock of this surprise, I went to the center of the stage and Marina pinned the medal on me. I humbly accepted this honor in the name of my country.

Phone and Photo Healings

After being in healing for more than half a decade, I discovered that I could heal people merely by concentrating on their energy field, which I could pick up by either looking at a photo of them or concentrating on their name when I talked to them on the phone.

As many people wanted healings from me and found it inconvenient to travel the long distance to Encinitas, I decided to set aside one day a week just to do phone healings. The same energy is transferred to people via the phone as I would transfer to them if I were in the room with them. The phone conversation takes anywhere from five to fifteen minutes, but the healing continues until the person receives what he or she needs. When a client calls me, a contact is made with the person verbally and I start sending him or her the healing energy.

At this time it is important that the proper mental attitude is set, so I start off by asking the person to relax, close his or her eyes, and take a few deep breaths. It is important that the person is comfortable, whether sitting or reclining. After talking to the person a couple minutes to discuss any problems he or she might have, I tell the person to visualize a perfect, healthy body and know that the body naturally heals itself.

Then I go through some visualizations with the person, in conjunction with sending out the healing energy. At the end of this process I suggest that the person take some time, an hour or so, to go into a subliminal state and let the healing continue to work. When a doctor tells you to drink plenty of liquids and get plenty of rest, it is not just a cliché. The body is continually healing and renewing itself and it does that best when we enter the subliminal state where the mind and the body are in a state of bliss. The body can then be in touch with its higher self without the conflicting distractions of the physical world.

I have been able to help many people through phone healings and there are some stories that stand out in my mind.

One day I was scheduled to work on a gentleman who was having problems with his right arm. As I listened to Jerome describing the physical symptoms, I began to send him the healing energy. After two or three minutes, I asked him to visualize his body in perfect health and then advised him to relax and try to fall asleep.

About a week later he called me.

"How is your arm?" I asked.

"Fine, fine," he said, "but that's not what I'm calling you about."

"Oh?"

"No, it so happens that when you were giving me the phone healing, my wife was listening on the extension. She was due for an eye operation the next morning, and when she went in for the surgery, the doctors couldn't find the problem. It had just disappeared. They were very surprised and confused. When she came home and told me, I thought I should call you and let you know."

"Well, I guess the energy I sent you zapped two birds with one healing. Tell your wife I am very happy for her."

This is an example of how the energy I send people goes to work wherever it is needed.

Another such phone healing comes to mind. I was giving an infant, Elly, a healing while her mother, Catherine, was holding her on her lap. The child had been born with a hole in her heart and every time she exhaled one could hear a "swishing" sound. As could be expected, this was causing a considerable amount of grief for the new parents. The doctors had told them to expect Elly to have a very short life. If she could survive the first few weeks, they would try corrective surgery; otherwise, she could be expected to die anytime.

After I did a healing on Elly, her mother, who was stressed out over the child's physical problem, decided to lie down and rest. She put Elly in her crib and they both ended up taking a nap. When Catherine woke up she went to Elly and picked her up out of her crib. As she held her she became aware that she no longer heard the "swishing" sound coming from her baby. She was overjoyed, but she thought that maybe her wishful thinking was playing tricks on her, so she decided to say nothing to her husband about it when he got home.

After being home for a while Sid, her husband, picked up their daughter to take her to her crib so that they could have a quiet dinner. He left the kitchen with Elly and was gone for a little longer than he should have been. He returned to the kitchen with a perplexed look on his face.

"You know, Catherine, when I put Elly down I couldn't hear that sound she makes. I stayed with her and put my head on her chest to see if it was quieter than usual, but I couldn't hear anything at all. What do you make of that?"

Catherine had a wide smile on her face. "I wasn't going to say anything unless you brought it up, but now that you've noticed it too, you've confirmed my hope. Let me tell you what happened today."

"What? What happened today?" asked Sid.

"I spoke to Gene Egidio. He did a healing on Elly by phone while she sat on my lap. When I'd finished talking to him, I was sleepy and decided to take a nap while Elly took hers. When I went in to take her out of her crib, I noticed that the 'swishing' sound was gone. Isn't it wonderful? It's a miracle!"

"*Incredible* is what it is," said Sid. "So now maybe she won't have to have surgery?"

"I'm hoping that's what the doctors will say."

After extensive medical testing, that is exactly what the doctors said. This was a very happy moment for the couple and I felt great about it.

Another happy ending for two young parents also comes to mind. One morning in January, I received a call from Europe. I heard a woman's voice with a heavy German accent.

"Hello, Gene. This is Gerta. Do you remember me? I had a healing with you last May in Frankfurt. I was pregnant at the time and you told me I was going to have a little boy."

"Ah, yes, I remember you."

"Gene, you were right, I did have a boy. Unfortunately, his heart is so badly damaged that the doctors only give him three or four days to live. He's now in intensive care."

I listened to Gerta's grief-stricken voice and began sending her and her little boy healing energy as I chatted with her for a couple of minutes.

"Gerta, I have just given you and your little boy some healing energy, and I'd like for you to call me tomorrow and let me know how your son is."

"Okay. I'll call you tomorrow. Good-bye, and thank you."

The next day, standing near the fax machine in my Santa Monica center, I watched a fax come through. I saw an image develop. It started with a set of eyes, then a button nose, a little mouth, and then the chin appeared on the fax paper. As I watched it come out of the machine, I saw there was a short note just under the chin. It read:

Dear Gene,
I just thought you might like to know that my son is doing

fine and the doctors are very baffled. You see, they can no longer find any evidence that there is anything wrong with his heart.

> *Much love,*
> *Gerta*

I've hung this faxed photo of the child on my wall in my Encinitas center as a reminder of these good moments.

One day a gentleman by the name of Elmer was scheduled to have a phone healing with me. In the phone conversation he mentioned that his sister was very sick and in a lot of pain. I told him I would concentrate on her and see what I could do to help.

The next day the phone rang and it was Elmer. "Gene, I want to tell you what I just learned."

"Okay, shoot, what news did you receive?" I asked.

"Well, you said you would concentrate on my sister and see what you could do to help; so, as I was curious, I called her to see if she was feeling any better, and she said, 'It's funny you happened to call. I'm feeling much better today, and you won't believe what happened last night.'

" 'Try me,' I said.

"She told me, 'Well, I must have slipped into a dream state. I saw a man standing at the foot of my bed holding on to my feet. He smiled at me and I knew he was there to help. When I woke this morning the pain was gone.'

" 'Well, what did this man look like? Can you describe his physical features?' I asked her.

" 'Oh, he was a large man with brown twinkling eyes and dark hair. And he had a mustache.'

"As I listened to her describing this man's physical features, I realized that she was describing *you*, and it was such a shock that I dropped the phone."

"I'm glad she's feeling better," I said casually.

"Yeah, but Gene, you don't understand, my sister lives in Thailand!"

"Well, we mustn't let a little physical distance stand in the way. After all, her energy is in the universe. The fact that she is in Thailand instead of California really isn't an issue for me."

"Oh, right," said Elmer, "I wasn't aware that you could heal long distance."

"Elmer, I healed *you* long distance. It's true the distance between us was shorter than the distance between me and your sister, but nevertheless the same principle was at work."

"Well, Gene, it was kind of peculiar, but I am glad you were able to help her," he said.

"Good. Enough said," I responded.

Photo healings work the same way as phone healings, and by this time, I probably have thousands of photos hanging on the walls of my office. I decided to put them on the walls so the people in the photos would continue to receive the flow of energy that is present in my center, and this is especially heightened during the Friday night meditation class. I guess this would fall under the category of "maintenance" as it is ongoing, for becoming the picture of health is only part of the story. We have to maintain it, and that takes conscious effort. The body is the temple that houses our spirit and it needs to be taken care of and treated with love and respect.

The stories above have happy endings. Not every story has a happy ending, as many people wait until the eleventh hour to come to me. This is always very frustrating. As I look at their auras, I can see that their life force is weak and many times their energy field has been greatly damaged. If only I had had the opportunity to see these people before the damage was done to their bodies and their energy fields, it might have been possible for me to prevent their life force from ebbing. But again, because of the belief systems people have chosen to subscribe to, they have, out of fear and the belief that the rational mind and its ways are superior, chosen a path that made them a willing participant in engineering their own death. It makes me both angry and sad to observe these situations, as I realize there is much educating that needs to be done on all levels to change some of these archaic belief systems.

It is true that dying is a part of life. The old cliché that "we are born to die" is very true. This is the final stage of life. I call it graduation time. This is when our destiny and our free will come together and we leave this earth plane and our spirit takes over and we go into the light.

Kathelina

There are always a scattering of people on this planet at any given time who dedicate their lives to the service of others. One such person was Kathelina. I first met her through an herbalist in San Diego; he was using some of the various herbal combinations that Kathelina had put together for him to help people remedy their various ailments. The first day I was introduced to her, I shook her hand and I knew instantly she was someone very special. She was a short lady in her mid-fifties with streaks of gray in her hair and a warm smile. I could tell she had tremendous compassion in her heart, and I knew there wasn't anything she wouldn't try to do for you. She was very loving and she reached out to everyone.

Kathelina was Mexican by descent and angel by decree. She lived in Tecati, Mexico, in what I would call a very large cardboard box. She had married a Mexican man whose dream it was to build a church, and Kathelina, being the loving person she was, stood by him and helped him literally, every inch of the way. Although they were very poor people they somehow obtained a piece of land, and the first thing they decided to do was dig a well. They did this themselves, with the help of a few hand tools. They chiseled through rock, and dug through dirt and then chiseled through more rock. The well was about thirty feet deep. It was an amazing thing to see—I remember looking down into the well shaft when Kathelina had proudly shown me the well, and I could see stretches of rock five to six feet deep, and these two people had chiseled through this rock in order to have a well! Every pick of the chisel had been an act of love for them. The feat was incredible and the work must have taken a great number of man hours, but because of their love and determination they successfully completed this task. Then they ran out of everything, including physical energy, but not willpower to see the dream to completion. Kathelina's husband got sick, but he continued to work and together they did manage to get the frame of the church up before he passed away.

Kathelina had incredible intuitive abilities. She could look at you, shake your hand, and tell you what kind of oil filter you had on your car. She was an herbalist in the true sense of the word. She had an innate understanding of herbs and their uses, although she never had any formal schooling. She was used to helping people and her knowledge of plants and their uses was just one of the ways she helped. Because of the incredible amount of love and compassion she had in her heart, she took in every homeless child who crossed her path. They were all her children, and they all called her Mother. She would go without food for herself in order to have something to feed these children.

I was so taken with her tremendous outpouring of love to humanity that I told her I would like to visit her in Tecati. She didn't speak any English, but through an interpreter she told me she would be glad to have me come to her home.

I had only been healing for two years, and I was still trying to understand what I was doing in the scheme of things. At that time I kept running into people like Kathelina. Because of her compassion and deep understanding of all things spiritual, I felt she might be able to throw some light on my situation, so one Saturday I decided to take a ride to Tecati with a Spanish-speaking friend. I had no directions, and after I crossed the border I tried to make out the road signs. When I got about fifteen miles from the border I saw a dirt road and although there was no sign, my intuition told me to turn onto it. As I got to the top of the first hill, I could see the skeleton of a building, so I decided I must be heading in the right direction. When I got to the bottom of the hill I saw several large cardboard and wooden boxes. I guess you could call them structures, but I should probably not upgrade them to such.

As I drove on, I spotted Kathelina standing in the center of this scattering of boxes. There were probably thirty to forty children around her. I didn't count them, but I knew they were considerable in number. There were children on crutches, there were children with their arms in bandaged slings, and there were some who were sick and were lying on the ground. Others were standing around watching Kathelina.

I stopped the car and got out. She was totally oblivious to my arrival. I walked over to the area where she was and watched her working on some of the sick children. Finally she became aware of my presence, turned and flashed a warm and compassionate smile, and started speaking in Spanish. I assumed she was telling me about the children, as she kept pointing to first one and then another of them. My Spanish vocabulary consists of about half a dozen words, but as I looked at her and watched her I became aware that I understood every word she was saying; it was as if she were speaking to me in English. I remarked about that to the person who was with me, but she wasn't having the same experience and couldn't understand a word Kathelina was saying.

As we went through the day, I saw that the sick children weren't the only ones Kathelina was working with. There were other children in each of the cardboard and wooden structures, and there were also children out in the surrounding fields working in their vegetable garden. She also had a few chickens. These people had just the bare essentials, no electricity or running water, but there was a feeling of peace and safety here, and as she worked with the children she was pouring out much love to them.

It was a hot day and she could tell I had become thirsty. That was when I was introduced to the well. She smiled and motioned for me to follow her. She took me to the well she and her husband had dug. She drew up a bucket of water and filled a cup and handed it to me. It was very cold and tasted very good. I had never, before or since, tasted such good water; it tasted like roses smell.

As I continued to get acquainted with Kathelina, I found out that she had rose water that she used to heal people. She had learned to extract the essence from roses and put it in her water and then she blessed it. I found out that she used the rose water to heal all the children.

The children in the vicinity knew enough to come to Kathelina when they were sick or without a place to stay, and she always took them in. Now I realized why I had seen a lone child here and there walking on the highway: They were en route to Kathelina and, sure enough as I looked up, I saw more children walking down the dirt road headed in our direction. She saw them too and smiled and waved to them.

There were other people coming to Kathelina, people from the United States as well as her own countrymen. The word was out that she could heal, and they all came to experience her healing powers. I spent the day with Kathelina and as I watched her going from child to child and working with practically no resources, I felt there was something I had to do for this woman.

"I would like to do something for you," I said. "Is there something you need that I can help you with?"

She smiled at me and said, "You'll know what to do when it's time."

When evening came I bid Kathelina good-bye, got in my car, and headed back to the States. I was totally consumed with Kathelina and what I could do to help this beautiful saint. This lady had totally dedicated her life to helping humanity without asking for anything in return, and I wanted to do something for her.

Back in the States I started collecting used clothing and anything else I could get my hands on. Three weeks later I went back to Tecati with a trunk full of clothes in my back-seat. I had also collected pots and pans and even some old electric toasters. As I turned up the dirt road to Kathelina's, it hit me: Why did I bring her electric toasters? This woman had no electricity!

When I pulled up, Kathelina looked up and waved to me.

I got out and started getting the things I had collected out of the car. Suddenly I was surrounded by curious children. Kathelina made her way to the car, spoke to the children, and they scattered.

"I brought you some used clothing and appliances," I said, "but I guess I got carried away. I forgot you don't have electricity and I brought you some electric toasters and frying pans."

Kathelina smiled as she looked at the goods. As she started speaking to me in Spanish, again I understood every word she was saying. "It is good you brought the electric toasters and pans," she said, "for I can sell them and use the money to buy the things the children here need." Her smile conveyed a warm appreciation of my effort.

This routine continued for a good length of time. Every couple of months I would get some clothes and shoes and appliances together and take them to Kathelina. Although I knew I was able to help her, I felt that what I was doing was not enough, so about six months down the road I got another idea. I was going to try to bring Kathelina to the States. This way she could work on the people who couldn't get to her in Tecati.

I wanted her to have a place to do healings and I knew I could get an audience of fifty to seventy-five people. I also knew a group this size would be no problem for her because her keen insights made it possible for her to work very quickly. After I got this put together I went to Tecati and asked her if she would be willing to come to the States and do healings. I seriously doubt if Kathelina even had the word "no" in her vocabulary. When I explained the situation to her she smiled warmly and agreed to make her services available.

I told her I would be down at a certain time to pick her up and I told her to bring her herbs and rose water.

She smiled and nodded.

When the day came to get Kathelina, I drove to Tecati and what I saw astounded me. There was Kathelina sitting in the midst of a bunch of potato sacks full of herbs. These were not tiny sacks but sacks about four feet long, absolutely stuffed with herbs.

"Kathelina, they will never let us over the border with all these sacks."

She smiled her big warm smile and said nothing. Instead, she picked up a jar of her rose water and one of the sacks and started toward the car.

"Okay, let's put these things in the car and see what happens," I said.

When we came to the border, the border guard came over to the car and leaned over. I took a deep breath as he looked at me and then at Kathelina, who sat surrounded with her sacks of herbs and jars of rose water. He looked at her and she smiled at him. He waved us through.

I was amazed and speechless. After we crossed the border, I looked in the rearview mirror and there sat Kathelina smiling.

"Kathelina," I said, "I don't believe this."

She continued smiling, and then I realized what she had done: She had communicated telepathically with the border control guard that what she had with her was needed to help people improve their health.

This was a first for me. I had never seen such a helpful border control guard in my life, nor had I seen one with such a big friendly smile.

We finally reached our destination and Kathelina immediately went to work. Without saying a word, she started intuitively dispensing her herbs to people; she was literally giving them away. I watched this for a while and finally I decided to intervene.

"You know, you have to help this lady out, because she takes care of hundreds of children, so please give her a donation," I said to those receiving her herbs and rose water.

I passed a little basket around the auditorium, and people began giving her small donations of whatever they felt they could afford. At the end of the day I put it all together and gave the money to her.

She looked at me, surprised. "What is this?"

"This is what the people here today gave you."

She looked at me and then at the money. "This is mine?"

"Yes, it is," I replied.

"What did I do to get this?"

I was totally taken aback. Finally I found my voice and said, "You gave a service to these people today; you helped them, and they gave you this in return."

"Will you hold the money for me?"

"No," I said, "I want to give you the money. I know you have many uses for it."

As I watched her I realized she was totally unaccustomed to handling money and she was actually afraid of it. She didn't even want it in her hands.

During the course of the afternoon and evening as she

went through the auditorium working with each person individually, she went through every situation imaginable. She had the usual couple of wisecrackers and there were those who made some smirky and disrespectful remarks.

"Just what are your qualifications to be doing this work? What schooling did you have?" asked one gentleman.

Kathelina turned and replied simply, "I have had the schooling of life."

This man just couldn't let well enough alone. He then asked her to solve a calculus problem. She accommodated him and spat out the answer without blinking an eye.

I don't know whether she knew what she was saying or not, but it was the right answer, for the guy's look of disbelief acknowledged that. After that he put his head down and never said another word.

Kathelina was a hit there and the people asked her to come back.

I drove her back to Mexico that night. It was late when we got to Tecati, about one in the morning. Kathelina invited me to stay over, which meant that she was going to give up her box springs. I wouldn't hear of that, so I compromised. I told her I would stay, but I would sleep in the car. I told her I needed to awaken very early as I had business to take care of in San Diego the next day. She smiled. We said our good nights and I got in the car and put the seat down and went to sleep. I was awakened a few hours later by a rooster's crow. When I opened my eyes I saw one of her children with a rooster in his arms; this was their alarm clock and they were making sure I was awake so I could get an early start. By this time the car was surrounded by children and there was Kathelina standing there with a tin coffee cup. She motioned for me to take the cup. I took the cup and drank. It was water from Kathelina's well. Somehow or other she had found a way to heat the water; that was breakfast.

As we were saying our good-byes, I looked up and saw a

car coming down the hill toward Kathelina's cardboard box. When the car stopped, a man and his wife got out and approached Kathelina.

As the husband could speak Spanish, he told Kathelina that his wife had a dropped uterus and the doctors had told her she had to have surgery. She was in much pain and needed help.

Kathelina smiled and extended her hand to the woman. Then she turned back and motioned to me to follow them. Kathelina took the woman into her cardboard box. There she had a chair and a table. She motioned for the woman to sit on the table. As the woman sat Kathelina began unwinding the large scarf she had around her neck. She walked over to the woman, took hold of her feet, and literally lifted her legs up in the air in an "L" position. While she held the woman's feet in the air she wrapped the scarf around the woman's abdominal area very tightly. All the time Kathelina was smiling at her. When she finished wrapping the scarf around the woman, she spun her around on the table, put her feet on the ground, and motioned for her to stand up.

"How do you feel now?" Kathelina asked the woman.

The woman's expression was one of total surprise. "The pain is completely gone," she said. "How could you stop it so fast?"

Kathelina smiled. As I looked on, I was both impressed and amazed. By putting the woman in an "L" position she had put her uterus back in its normal place and then, by tying the scarf very tightly around the woman's abdominal area, she had seen to it that her uterus would be held in place. Primitive? Yes. Did it work? Yes. And best of all no knife had to be taken to the flesh.

My Interpreter

In my many travels I frequently go to lands where English is not spoken. As that is the only language I speak, I have the need for interpreters to translate for me so I can communicate with the people I work on. In the early days I would ask for one interpreter, but I quickly found out that one was not sufficient. Because of the amount of energy these people were receiving by constantly being in close proximity to me, I would get ready to talk to one of my clients and when I turned to the interpreter to do the translating, I would discover he or she had nodded off. This was quite a drawback, so I finally decided to have three or four interpreters on hand. When one had the need to sleep, I could pick up with another where the first one left off. This worked out much better.

While I was in Germany recently, I happened to mention to one of my interpreters, Johann, that I was writing a book. I asked him if he would like to share his impressions of what he had experienced when he worked with me and the passage that follows is what he observed.

I am a computer analyst for an international company. I've always had an insatiable interest in many things, so I have read extensively on many topics. One of the things I have found the most fascinating is the many dimensions of the mind.

When Gene Egidio, an American healer, came to Germany for the first time, I decided to go have a session with him, purely out of curiosity. I didn't really know what to expect, and I was quite frankly skeptical that anything unusual would happen, but when I arrived at the auditorium where he was going to be, I noticed that there was an unusually positive atmosphere. When Gene entered the room, the first physical signs of something very special going on manifested in the form of people weeping, which represented to me a sign of people relieving pent-up emotional stress. After he was introduced he did an Open Eye Meditation and I knew that this man was unique. I saw an aura, or misty halo of light, around people's heads for the first time in my life! This is crazy, I thought. As I looked at the auras around people I realized how very much it looked like the aureole on the old Christian paintings. Could it be possible that a man equipped with heavenly powers was wandering around here today just like in the old days? I thought to myself that maybe those long-forgotten painters of Christian icons did paint what they saw; it wasn't made up or symbolic as we are told by authorities today. As I continued to look at this phenomenon I said to myself, Man this is real!

And then my rational intellectual side started working to try to figure out what tricks could have been used to cause this sight. My rational mind was having a great deal of trouble accepting something I had definitely seen but could not explain. Even though I retained a certain amount of skepticism I decided not to let it keep me away from new experiences, so I decided to take this new experience as far as I could. As I was bathing in this positive atmosphere I was becoming aware of a reality much larger than what we are usually experiencing and as I looked around I became aware that what we consider to be reality was just a small part of something much larger. When I looked at the other people in the room to see what their reactions were I realized that we had been put into contact with a view of the real world that most of us had never been consciously aware of.

As I thought about what was going on, I became so impressed with what I saw and felt that I found myself comparing Gene with the wise men from the biblical age, for the impact of this new reality was so overwhelming. The reactions of the other people in the room were also impressive. Some had entered altered states of mind, some were smiling radiantly, and some were releasing emotional stress by crying. Seeing all these different reactions I felt very happy for these people.

Needless to say I decided to have a hands-on healing after what I had experienced, and that too was a rewarding experience. When Gene touched my body it felt like a warm liquid stream of love pouring into me. I felt the warmth all through me and I entered into a subliminal state which lasted for about an hour and a half.

Later I learned what that warm feeling was capable of doing. It touched every problem that needed attention. For instance, I was relieved of the pain of a migraine within a few seconds. Not even a good painkiller could do that trick without giving you some undesirable side effects such as dizziness.

After this first meeting with Gene I decided I would like to support him and I volunteered to help him in any way I could when he returned to Germany. I did little things here and there the next time he came to Germany, and finally I started interpreting for him. It was in that position that I learned a lot about what Gene was doing as I got to see many wonderful things happen to people firsthand. I think you could call some of the things that happen to people when Gene is around miracles. If you think that miracles only happened two thousand years ago, you should take a look at some of the things that are possible now, and I think you might find yourself a bit astonished and pleasantly pleased.

Even though Gene has been healing for several years, he is not floating above the ground and above the problems common *to ordinary people. In my opinion he is a human developed to his full potential and that includes his behavior towards the people in need of help. He does what he can do to help within the cosmic laws, laws that many of us have lost touch with or forgotten completely.*

Some of the physical healings I witnessed were most attractive and impressive to see. But for sure, even more important are those healings that are not visible on the outside, but when you look into the eyes of the people who are experiencing the energy Gene sends, you can feel the larger impact these healings are going to have on the people's lives. It is impossible to estimate the total consequences of such a healing process when a whole community experiences it. I think it was once said that if only a hundred men would change themselves, the whole world would change.

Although most people, myself included, like to experience the transfer of energy by direct touch, Gene can send this same energy to any spot on the planet, for this transfer is not confined to space and time as we know it. For instance, Gene was able to heal a baby in Germany when he was in the States. I think this energy could best be described as the essence of pure love, life force, life energy, or heavenly light. But whatever description you choose, it is really good and it is capable of improving your health in the physical, emotional, mental, or spiritual body, for this pure love life force goes wherever it is needed.

Trying to describe the energy or its effects is like trying to describe a large building that you see only from one side. Somebody else sees it from another angle and delivers a different description. Many people have many different descriptions of what they experience. Most experience the energy as warmth, light, or sometimes coldness. It can create a sensation of tickling, vibration, steaming, floating, and even flight. Some people don't get any physical sensation at all. Sometimes they say they feel like they got loosened up inside, but invariably when everyone leaves the healing room they look much happier, and their shining eyes could light a festival hall.

The effects of Gene's energy are as many and diverse as the complaints of the people who come to him. There have been spontaneous healings of physical problems; there has been the start of slow healing processes; sometimes the healing process started several days later as the body needed some time to get going. When very sick people come to Gene for several sessions their health improves every day at a rate their loved ones can't believe. I saw cases of people so ill that conventional medicine had pretty much indicated the end was near, but within four sessions with Gene they were very much improved. Usually their families had the problem then of adapting to the thought that this was possible.

And then there are the people who keep themselves apart from the experience and refuse to participate, sometimes by being too curious or skeptical or just afraid. The experience Gene gives you is something you have to get involved in to fully experience it and receive its complete benefits. Otherwise, it would be like falling in love without getting involved. That way, you would never experience what it meant to be in love. There are also some cases where Gene can't help for whatever reasons. But wherever Gene is, there is a lot going on.

Gene's gift of being able to transfer wonderful energy is just a part of what he can do. He also has the gift of second sight and intuitive insights that can prove very helpful. He can give a person hints about ways to change his life for the better. He can see what your body needs. By one long look into your eyes he can tell where you have been and where you are heading. Sometimes his proposals sound strange but who cares, as long as they work. As he allows the universal energy to pass through him he has access to all the knowledge that was ever in his universe, stemming from all other cultures and time periods.

Now, if you are looking for a guru, you will be disappointed in Gene. Trying to put responsibility on him for your well-being, when it is truly your own, will not be tolerated by him. Gene says we have free will, and everybody has to get his own part done. He will, however, assist you in getting on the right path, but he doesn't take over. This is one quality for which I have great respect and admiration.

Sound like a declaration of love for Gene? Well, it is! I am grateful to Gene for all the light he is trying to bring into this world and I am also grateful to him for the love he has unselfishly given that was not attached to any conditions.

Again, thank you, Gene.

A Light Descends

During my travels to Egypt, I had agreed to do a meditation on the roof of one of the Egyptian temples at sunset during Ramadan, which is the Islamic month of fasting from sunrise to sunset. It was a rather nice time to be in Egypt, as a certain air of reverence and peace pervaded the country. We arrived at the temple and climbed up the stone stairs, just as the sun was setting. When we walked out onto the roof we could see the countryside of Egypt, the old and the new side by side with a bright red orange sunset. Ringing through the air was the chanting that was done at sunset and as I looked at the scene I thought to myself that this sight was the stuff dreams are made of. As the last streak of red left the sky, one could see the evidence of the twinkling stars, and I decided that since the temple was not lighted I had better do the meditation before it became totally dark. I had everyone form a circle and hold hands. After I gave the meditation I went around the circle and gave each person energy individually.

It was a beautiful place to do a meditation and the evening turned out to be very pleasant. After we got back to the States, I received a letter from June Tremer, one of the women on the tour, and she told me she wanted me to know what she had experienced during the meditation on the temple roof, and I would like to share her letter with you.

✻   ✻   ✻

Dear Gene,

I am writing to you to tell you about the experience I had with you and also to thank you for making it possible for, to put it mildly, it was a "show stopper."

When we arrived at the temple, I felt the structure itself was a marvel, and when we reached the roof and I looked at the countryside with the spectacular sunset as a backdrop, it was very inspiring. I felt the sensation of beauty all around me. As you started the meditation service, it was pleasant, but I could not have guessed what I was about to witness until I happened to glance at you. I was standing almost directly in front of you, and as you instructed us to hold hands and be silent for a moment, I closed my eyes and bowed my head. After a moment I looked up and I saw a pool of white light descending out of the sky. As I watched it I realized it was homing in on you. Finally it touched the floor of the temple directly behind you. As I continued to look at this phenomenon it began to take the form of a human about a foot to a foot and a half taller than you, and it stood directly behind you. It had no features, it was just a silhouette of light. You were concentrating solely on the meditation, and it looked as though you were totally unaware of what was going on directly behind you. I wondered if I should interrupt you, but before I could say anything the light form walked into your body. It was such a beautiful merging, very smooth and natural. When you started the meditation I had seen a purplish glow around you but after the light body merged with you, your aura shot out about eighteen inches from your body, and it turned a golden color with twinges of purple, blue, and white.

When you came around the circle and gave each of us energy I felt a strong electric tingle run from the top of my head down my spine to my feet. The experience caused my whole body to vibrate and I felt as if every cell in my body was twinkling like the stars overhead.

This was such a beautiful sight to see, that it is etched in my memory forever. Just knowing that something like that is possible has given me a great deal of happiness and restored my waning hope in all things good. Thank you so much for allowing me to have this experience.

June

My Experience with Divine Protection

It was during the mid-1980s that I started getting an intuitive feeling to go to Auschwitz. I ignored it for a while, but then one morning as I was preparing to do healings in my center in Santa Monica I started getting the message again. As I sat in my chair relaxing, the message started getting stronger and stronger. It was telling me that there were many tortured souls lingering in the vicinity of the Nazi concentration camps and that I needed to go there and release the souls, as I had done in Leningrad. After listening to the message for a few minutes, I glanced at my watch and realized it was time to start my day, so I shut the message out of my mind and started doing the healings that my assistant had scheduled. During the course of the day I noticed that almost all of my clients were Jewish. One of my close friends, Betty Scalar, also Jewish, was talking to me about her mother and family and spiritual things. After chatting with her for a while, I decided to tell her about the message I had been receiving all morning.

"Betty," I said, "I've been getting an intuitive feeling about something I would like you to comment on."

"Oh, what's that?" she asked.

"I'm getting the message that I need to go to the concentration camps in Poland and release the tortured souls there so the Jewish people all over the world can experience more peace. What do you think about that message?"

"Gene," Betty said, "you've listened to your inner voice before and it has always been right, so I would think that you should listen to it now."

"Betty, I'm just barely able to keep this place going. If I leave for a couple of weeks, I won't be able to keep up with the rent, not to mention the traveling expenses."

She looked at me and smiled. As her time was up, she said good-bye and left.

The next day as I was having lunch, in walked Betty.

"Gene, I'd like to help out with your trip to the concentration camps," she said as she took an envelope out of her purse and handed it to me.

"That is very generous of you, but I haven't decided if I am going to make the trip yet, so I can't accept anything from you."

She stood there looking at me and then she pressed the envelope into my hand. "Here, you use this for some of the expenses," she said and then she walked out of the room.

I guess she spread the word that I was going to visit the camps, because suddenly everyone was making donations to the cause.

Inwardly I knew I was going to go, but the rational side of me hadn't accepted this decision yet.

One morning as I was driving to the center, I found myself stopping at a travel agent in the vicinity.

"How can I help you?" said the lady in the travel agent's office as I entered.

"How much would a round-trip to Poland be?"

"Oh, I can find you a good bargain," she said. "The fall rates are still in effect."

She handed me an estimate on a slip of paper. I thanked her and headed to my center.

After going through this procedure a half-dozen times, I

finally found a cheap airfare that made it feasible to under-
take this trip. I knew I needed to go to Poland first and then
up through Germany, but I had no idea just where the specific locations were that I needed to go, so I decided to relax
and let my inner voice guide me to my destination.

The flight to Poland was very pleasant. When Inga and I
reached Warsaw, the last leg of our journey, I felt as though
I was in the U.S.S.R. again. The Russians were still occupy-
ing Warsaw, and there were Soviet troops everywhere.

My assistant, Bertha, who was European, had made contact with a lady who said she would help us. After we
claimed our luggage and went outside of the airport, there
stood this Polish lady in her mid-forties waiting for us with
a bouquet of flowers and a big smile.

She walked over to us and spoke to my assistant in
French. "You must be the Americans. I can tell by the way
you are dressed."

"Yes, we are from America," Bertha replied in fluent
French, then introduced us.

"Come, you must be tired. I want to invite you to my flat
for dinner and then we can talk about what you want to do."

"I need to go to several of the concentration camps, especially Auschwitz," I told her.

"Ah, it will take about two weeks to go there and get
back. You can't go by train because it does not run there.
The only way is by car."

"How much will that cost?"

"A lot, but they will rent you a car if you have an
American credit card."

"Well, I don't have an American credit card and I have to
make this trip in four days. That's all the time I have."

She shook her head. All the while we were discussing this
matter, I was observing the taxi drivers bidding for cus-
tomers. There was one driver who had a van. Boy, I thought
to myself, that would be great if we could get him to leave

Warsaw. We would have enough room in that for our luggage and ourselves. The man saw me looking at the van and walked over.

"I saw you looking at my van," he said. "Are you interested in seeing Warsaw? I speak English well enough that I can act as your tour guide and show you the city."

"How well do you know the surrounding country?" I asked.

"Pretty well. I am a native and I would be glad to drive you around."

"I need to go to Treblinka. How much would that cost?" I asked.

"Well, I would have to figure that out. I don't usually go on such long trips."

"Here's the deal: I have five hundred dollars and four days and I need to go to the concentration camps."

"Why do you want to go there? Those places are like something from bad dreams."

"I just feel that I must see these places," I answered.

"I don't think I can help you. The money you said you had is not enough. It would cost three times that amount to go there and a lot more time."

I stood there, saying nothing.

Finally he gazed up at the sky and then turned to me. "Okay, okay. I'll take you," he said.

I smiled and shook his hand and Inga and I began loading our luggage into the van. We told Bertha we would call her when we got back to Warsaw and off we went.

I told Thomas, the taxi driver, that we really needed to make the trip in three days. He shook his head and said, "Okay, I will try."

"Good enough," I said, and we sped away.

"Where do you want to sleep?" he asked as we headed out of Warsaw.

"We don't have time to sleep," I answered. "We will take

catnaps in the van. I don't want to lose any time and that means that we must be moving day and night.

"I have to start at Treblinka," I continued, "and then I want to go to Majdanek." Thomas looked at me mysteriously but said nothing.

After driving the better part of the day we reached Treblinka. Night had already fallen. It was pitch dark and the place had an eerie and desolate appearance. There was a barbed wire fence around the place and a watchtower looming up in the night. As I looked around, I spotted a huge monument and, as I circled it, I could feel the horrific terror the people had experienced here before they had died. When I got back to the point where I had started I stood there with my companions. Thomas was watching us, leaning against the hood of his car. Suddenly I looked down at my feet and saw a snake come out of the solid concrete monument, not from under it mind you, but actually *out* of it. How could a snake come out of solid concrete? I looked down again and saw it quickly cross my path and head into the woods near the monument. As the three of us watched the snake head for the forest, I intuitively knew that the snake was the physical sign that the souls had been released.

We got back into the van and headed for the next camp. We drove all night and arrived early the next morning. There were rows and rows of foundations from the barracks that had once stood there. In my mind's eye I could see that these buildings had entombed thousands of bodies, as they had been put into the foundations.

At this point we had been up for forty-eight hours, and we were beginning to feel grimy and grubby, so we gave in and went to a motel to freshen up and take a short snooze.

As I slept I had a dream that I was in the camp we were going to visit next, Birkenau. This was the camp where people were driven into showers that ran cyanide gas. In my dream I was part of a group being packed into a covered truck. I could hear little screams and gasps as the rear door slammed shut. As we were being driven, the engine's exhaust was being fed back into the truck, its stench filling the air. It was so crowded that one couldn't fall over, but I could see people's heads dropping to their shoulders. One person turned and looked at me. The face I saw was the face of my grandson. With this shock I woke up and sat straight up in bed. I was too disturbed to go back to sleep. Earlier in this journey I had received a foreboding message that if I proceeded with this trip something terrible would happen to my grandson. I was very concerned, but I knew that I must take this journey to its completion.

When it became daylight I asked Thomas to take us to Auschwitz.

"I'm not sure which way to go, but I know it's only two or three kilometers from here," he responded.

"Just follow those birds," I said, pointing to a flock overhead. "They will take us there."

"Why the birds?" he asked.

"Because the birds signify the release of souls, and they will show us how to get there."

"Okay," he said.

I knew he thought I was a nut, but he nevertheless followed the birds. After going through a maze of roads we ended up at the entrance to Auschwitz. The words *Arbeit Macht Frei*, which Inga told me means "Work Makes Free," were inscribed over the gate.

The buildings and barbed wire fences at Auschwitz have been preserved as the Museum of Martyrdom, so they attract crowds of tourists.

As we pulled to a halt and got out of the van, Thomas pointed to a sign and said, "We have to go this way." He nodded in the direction of the groups of people who were already there.

"No," I said, "we have to go in the opposite direction."

"That direction will take us into a dense forest."

"Nevertheless, my intuition is telling me to go in this direction."

He shrugged his shoulders and we started away from the people. After we'd walked a short distance, we rounded a bend and there was a hole in the fence. We crawled through it and there we were, standing in front of three identical buildings.

These were the buildings that had the ovens in them. We were alone, so I was able to have the quiet atmosphere I needed to do my work.

We went into the building that housed the ovens and the heaviness of energy there was so dense and laden with sorrow it could knock you over. I put my hand on one of the ovens and the trolley that brought the bodies. As my hand lay there, I realized that many souls had been put in these ovens while they were still alive. This was too much for my companions so they left the building.

I stayed until I could no longer feel the deep sadness and the density of the energy, and then I went outside. As I approached my traveling companions, Inga looked at me and smiled.

"Do you smell something?" she asked me.

I took a whiff of the air and realized that it was filled with the odor of the incense that I normally burn when I do healings in my center. This was the signal to me that my work was finished.

"Okay, Thomas," I said, "that was the last place I was directed to go, so get us back to Warsaw as fast as you can."

We all got back into the van and Thomas sped off. He was driving down the highway at an excessive speed, passing everything in sight. After a while we got behind a large truck that was lumbering down the road. Thomas kept trying to pass, but every time he pulled out there were oncoming vehicles. Finally in exasperation he pulled out and there, not more than five car lengths away, was a school bus. The cars behind us had closed in and Thomas couldn't get back into the lane behind the truck. I was sitting in the front seat with him and I thought, This isn't going to be a good experience, but just as we reached the point where we should have hit the school bus head-on, the bus moved literally sideways off the road and there, suddenly, was just enough space for us to go through. It was as if someone had taken hold of the bus and slid it over.

As we passed the bus, I could see that the expression on the driver's face was one of stunned disbelief. I was amazed at what had happened, as was everyone else, because vehicles just can't go sideways. For me that is one of the most direct interventions of divine protection I have ever seen or experienced.

We reached Warsaw in the early dawn and we were a sorry sight. We called Bertha and told her we were back and we were going to go to a hotel and freshen up and sleep.

"I have completed my work here, and I just want to let you know that we will be leaving in the morning," I told her.

"Oh, no," said Bertha, very disappointed. "I have been telling everyone you are here and a lot of people want to experience a healing."

I got off the phone and told my companions what Bertha had said. My companions shrugged their shoulders and said, "Great."

"I'm glad you feel that way," I said, "because I told her I'd do healings for the next two days."

Thomas the driver was still with us. "I would like to invite you to my home for lunch," he said to us. "After what I have seen in the last three days, I wouldn't take a penny from you if I could afford not to, but I need the money for the upkeep of my van and to support my family."

"I understand," I said, handing him the five hundred dollars, which was all I had budgeted for my transportation costs.

That night we went to Bertha's apartment. After a pleasant evening meal, she took us to the auditorium she had reserved. It was no larger than a medium-sized living room, and when we walked in it was wall-to-wall people. As I glanced around, I estimated that she must have gotten about three hundred people together. They didn't know what to expect so they started singing when we entered the room, and they didn't stop until I asked them to be quiet. I gave a little talk and did the Open Eye Meditation. Then I lined up ten catchers, to stand behind the people I was doing healing on. I instructed everyone in the room to form a line and come up and take a place in front of one of the catchers. This made it possible for me to do a healing on every person in the crowd. Because the room was so small I could only do ten people at a time. It took longer than it should have, but when I saw their reaction I knew the time was well spent. Although these people weren't sure what to expect, it was obvious they had been waiting for this experience. They were very accepting and appreciative of what I did and told me they'd be waiting for my return.

Where the Angels Live

Angels have a history as old as human civilization itself. Some say they are merely figments of our imagination, while others say they are real. Yet others say they are aliens from another civilization. Although it is acknowledged that there are evil angels as well as good angels, the most popular notion about angels is that each person has a guardian angel, and that angel is always with the person for protection and to help the person with any problems that may arise. The guardian angel loves the person unconditionally regardless of what that person does or does not do. Many artists have rendered their visions of angels and the angel image is very broad, as can be seen from the many different ways they have been painted. People usually think of angels as doing good things to help humanity and sometimes it is thought that they work through humans. It is thought that the angels touch the heartstrings of humans and they in turn take on the qualities the angels are known to have. Christel, Angelika, Agi, and Gerda are four such people I had the privilege of meeting while on a healing trip to Nuremberg, Germany.

When I left for a healing trip to Europe, I was scheduled to go to Switzerland, Russia, and England. After leaving Switzerland, I went to St. Petersburg in Russia. On the first morning there I received a fax from England saying they were canceling my visit. No explanation. Nothing. Just a note saying "We are informing you that we are canceling your forthcoming trip."

I had felt good about going to a new place, and I was disappointed about this sudden change in plans. But, as it turned out, the next day I received a fax from my office in Encinitas saying that Nuremberg would gladly take me for the time slot England did not want. Since I was already in Europe, I decided to go to Nuremberg. When I arrived at the airport in Frankfurt, there were four people waiting to drive me to Nuremberg. As they all spoke English, we were able to have a pleasant conversation as we drove to Nuremberg. They said they were collecting used clothing and shoes to take to people who were in need, and I commented in passing that it was nice to help others. At that time they didn't tell me where the people in need were located.

As they were interested in what I did, I invited them to the Open Eye Meditation I was planning to do that night and they said they would be there.

When I give the Open Eye Meditation in a community for the first time, I give a little talk about myself and what I do and then I explain the purpose of the Open Eye Meditation. I had a full house that evening and so I quickly passed around the room and gave everyone a sampling of the energy. As I was working my way down the line of people, I spotted Christel, Angelika, Agi, and Gerda, and I could tell they were enjoying the experience. When I reached the end of the line there was a woman in a wheelchair, a paraplegic, I found out later. I gave her energy and she began rising up from the chair. I instantly sensed that she would probably be able to regain considerable movement facility, so I invited her to come to a healing session I was going to be conducting the next day.

She came and the same thing happened when I worked on her; her body would arc up and she would nearly lift off the table. Each time I gave her the healing energy she would lift up off the table a little higher, and I began to get a sense of exercises she should be doing to increase her mobility. I told her husband to come in and videotape the different positions I wanted her to put her body in every day. She was a strong-willed woman and, although she was paralyzed, she made a concentrated effort to visualize the movements in her mind as I described them to her and then she would physically try, with my help, to do what I was describing to her. I let her stay in the healing room until the last person had left so she could continue receiving the healing energy and when I finally went over to her to talk to her she was crying.

"I knew the moment I saw you that I was going to get better," she said, smiling through tears.

"Why did you know that?" I asked.

"I was in a very serious car accident five years ago in Spain," she said. "I was in a coma for a long time and during that time I saw a man with your facial features standing by my bedside smiling at me. When I saw you, I recognized you from the dream I had of you while I was in my coma and I knew I was supposed to be here."

And I nearly went to England, I thought to myself. At that instant I realized the truth in a favorite saying of mine, namely that we are always in the right place at the right time.

We had many good healings in Nuremberg and finally on the last day my four organizers came to me.

"We are going to say good-bye now, as we won't be here in the morning when you leave. We are leaving in a few minutes and we plan to take turns driving all night so we will be in the vicinity of where we are going when daylight breaks."

"Oh, where are you going?"

"Bosnia."

"Bosnia? Why are you going there? Bombs and bullets are flying!"

"Yes, well, we either go there or to Greece every two weeks to take things to the people who have nothing."

"You mean you drive across the border into Bosnia without any problems?"

"Yes, it is not a problem to get into the country at certain points."

"But Bosnia is a war zone," I protested.

"Yes, and the people there really need a lot of things, so we take clothes and shoes and anything else we can find that we think they can use."

"How did you get started doing this?"

"Oh, it was to be a Christmas present for the poor children who live in Menithi, a slum in Athens," said Christel.

"How did a Christmas present for Greek children land you in Bosnia?" I asked.

Christel continued, "As I said, a friend of ours told us that a woman who takes care of children in the Menithi area was in urgent need of shoes for the children. It was in 1993 that Angelika and I decided to try to make a difference, so we asked everyone we ran into to give us old shoes for the children in Menithi. Some of the people, like Gerda and Agi, not only gave us shoes but volunteered to help us distribute them, so we loaded my van and headed to Greece. This was to be a one-shot deal, but when we got there we saw that not only the children, but other people as well, needed much more than just shoes.

"It was while we were there that we met Lipan, a twenty-one-year-old Kurd who had no feet. Although he had been given artificial limbs, the fit was bad and he could only walk with great pain. When we saw this we knew that we had much work to do, so we came back to Nuremberg and started raising money so he could have proper-fitting prostheses. This, of course, opened a huge can of worms. Through Lipan we were put in touch with many people in Kurdistan with the same problem as he."

"What you're doing is truly remarkable," I said. "If more people would reach out to those who are less fortunate, life would probably get easier on this planet."

"Yes, our one-time effort to help the orphans in Greece was like putting a Band-Aid on a patient who had just had surgery. It just wasn't enough."

"Well, I'm very impressed—not only that you're helping these people but that you're willing to put your lives on the line to do so," I acknowledged, after listening to their story.

"Yes, well, when you get there and see what's needed, you forget about the danger and just start doing what you can to help," said Christel.

"And we've also made inroads into getting medical help to victims who've had their legs and arms blown off," said Agi. "These people need to be fit for prostheses. They have nothing and they really need help."

"And we've been lucky enough to find some doctors who are willing to donate their time free of charge to help these people," Gerda pitched in. "We take up donations to get the money for the materials for the prostheses."

I was very glad to have met them. Their enthusiasm was refreshing in an age when so many people are callous. I listened to them telling about their venture with delight.

"We have made it possible for some of these people to have a better quality of life," said Angelika.

"Well, once again, your efforts are to be commended," I said.

"You know, we're just ordinary people taking tiny steps, one after the other, but if enough people will do this the face of the world could change."

"Very true," I said. "Well, I would like to help too. What can I do?"

"Any help you can give us will be greatly appreciated."

As I thought about these brave people, I could not imagine the courage it must take to go into a heavily mined war-torn country to do what these four ladies were doing. They had enough compassion in their hearts to reach out to others regardless of the dangers they might encounter themselves. They were going where everyone else feared to tread and they were touching lives in a positive and loving way, for the people in this war-torn country don't think the war will ever end.

Christel, Agi, Gerda, Angelika, and the other volunteers receive no money for this. They all work full-time jobs and pay their own way to do this work in their spare time. They continue to reach out to those in need and constantly look for ways to help people who are less fortunate than they.

When we left Nuremberg my faith in mankind had been lifted tremendously. Although these people were not healers per se, they were certainly doing healing work, for they were healing the emotional scars, as well as helping by obtaining the necessary material goods needed for survival. And, most important of all, they were giving these people a glimmer of hope, as well as letting them know that there were people who still cared.

To embrace humanity with a loving heart and compassion in your soul and walk with your hand extended out to your fellow man is a way to live that will surely be rewarded. These people are doing a tremendous job of walking on that path.

By doing everything they can to help others, they are doing something for themselves, for it is in the service of others that we truly find ourselves.

When I first heard their story I commented that surely the angels must live in Nuremberg but, upon reflection, I realized that the angels live in the hearts of all brave people.

Epilogue

Dear gentle ones, open your hearts and your minds, for this is indeed the way that shall lead you into a higher concept of who you are and who your God is. As a man thinketh in his heart so he becomes, for a man is literally what he thinks.

The body is merely a servant of the mind, for a thought must happen before the body can carry it out. I always say, *Keep your hands firmly upon the helm of your thoughts, for you hold the key to your condition.* Always listen carefully to your inner voice and let your heart embrace that which it can accept. Know that when your heart, intuition, and intellect are all three in agreement you are on the path to making right choices.

You live in your consciousness, for there is nowhere else you can live. When you confirm that you are one with good, strength, health, love, prosperity, and the light, you fulfill a spiritual law. Many people ask me, "Well, what are the spiritual laws?" The *word* by you is law. The *word* of you creates, and the *word* of you molds. It is wise to practice holding perfect images, as you must express on the outer that which you visualize internally. A favorite saying of mine is, *Where your attention goes, your energy flows,* and it is this energy that builds what you visualize.

How do you come to the realization of a certain truth? One way is to meditate on that truth daily for five minutes.

Sit down every day and quietly affirm it a hundred times over and let nothing else enter into your mind. This one truth shall soon become a reality. Every cell in your body will be on fire with the truth of it. It will no longer be something you believe; it will be something you know. All things are in man for the perfect working out of the pattern of his life on this earth.

You may pray much and you may dream of things you want to do. Your world is made up of these things you dream of, but unless you put these things into action, your prayer goes amiss. Action is the only way that your dreams will come to fruition. Without action you are stagnant.

So, gentle ones, let your consciousness expand, open your heart, and continue on your path with your hands extended to those you meet. Be that loving and compassionate person you really are, because there is no one else like you on this earth.

Know that you are love and you are loved.
Whoever you are, I love you.
Wherever you are, I give you my blessing.
Whatever you need, I will pray for you.
I leave you with my love and my peace.
So be it.
— Gene Egidio

"I have known Gene Egidio for many years. I am thoroughly impressed with his great care and deep compassion for those who are suffering. In Gene's tireless efforts around the world, he has eased the pain and brought wellness to countless people. I believe that in this time that we in the Buddhist tradition call the *Samsara* ocean of suffering, nothing could be of greater virtue."
—Steven Seagal, actor

"I have been experiencing chronic lower back pain for years. No conventional treatment had helped. After one session with Gene, my pain subsided. As a medical doctor, I was stunned. Gene's hands are a conduit for the Healing Power that is within all of us."
—Thomas D. Johnson, M.D., San Diego, California

"It is a great honor to have read WHOSE HANDS ARE THESE? To get a glimpse into the life of a dear friend who has clearly been given a gift of healing. This book is a gift to all the readers who will learn with every page about this gentle man who has left a beautiful mark on everyone he has come into contact with. The moment you look into his eyes, you realize that you are in the presence of a very special being. He heals with his hands and eyes...with a detour through the heart."
—Linda Gray, actress on *Dallas* and *Models, Inc.*

"Sometimes a book comes along at precisely the right moment in history. This is such a book. We are entering a new era of glorious, buoyant health and longevity that will be free of disease. Tomorrow's doctors will be trained in all the known arts of healing: allopathic, naturopathic, chiropractic, herbal, homeopathic, psychosomatic, spiritual, etc. Gene Egidio is one of the world's foremost spiritual healers. Entering the spiritual universe of Gene Egidio helps you to uncover something amazing, precious, and important about your Self."
—David Allen, Ph.D., author of *Harmony's House: A Storybook to Color*